The Jewel City

Its Planning and Achievement; Its Architecture, Sculpture, Symbolism, and Music; Its Gardens, Palaces, and Exhibits

Ben Macomber

1st WORLD
LIBRARY
Literary Society

The Jewel City

Ben Macomber

© 1st World Library – Literary Society, 2004
PO Box 2211
Fairfield, IA 52556
www.1stworldlibrary.org
First Edition

LCCN: 2004195201

Softcover ISBN: 1-4218-0111-6
Hardcover ISBN: 1-4218-0011-X
eBook ISBN: 1-4218-0211-2

Purchase *"The Jewel City"*
as a traditional bound book at:
www.1stWorldLibrary.org/purchase.asp?ISBN=1-4218-0111-6

1st World Library Literary Society is a nonprofit
organization dedicated to promoting literacy by:

- Creating a free internet library accessible from any computer worldwide.
- Hosting writing competitions and offering book publishing scholarships.

**Readers interested in supporting literacy
through sponsorship, donations or
membership please contact:
literacy@1stworldlibrary.org
Check us out at: www.1stworldlibrary.ORG
and start downloading free ebooks today.**

The Jewel City
contributed by Tim, Ed & Rodney
in support of
1st World Library Literary Society

Contents

Introduction

No more accurate account of the Panama-Pacific International Exposition has been given than one that was forced from the lips of a charming Eastern woman of culture. Walking one evening in the Fine Arts colonnade, while the illumination from distant search-lights accented the glory of Maybeck's masterpiece, and lit up the half-domes and arches across the lagoon, she exclaimed to her companion: "Why, all the beauty of the world has been sifted, and the finest of it assembled here!"

This simple phrase, the involuntary outburst of a traveled visitor, will be echoed by thousands who feel the magic of what the master artists and architects of America have done here in celebration of the Panama Canal. I put the "artists" first, because this Exposition has set a new standard. Among all the great inter-national expositions previously held in the United States, as well as those abroad, it had been the fashion for managers to order a manufactures building from one architect, a machinery hall from another, a fine arts gallery from a third. These worked almost indepen-dently. Their structures, separately, were often beautiful; together, they seldom indicated any kinship or common purpose. When the buildings were completed, the artists were called in to soften their disharmonies with such sculptural and horticultural decoration as might be possible.

The Exposition in San Francisco is the first, though it will not be the last, to subject its architecture to a definite artistic motive. How this came about it is the object of the present book to tell, - how the Exposition was planned as an appropriate expression of America's joy in the completion of the Canal, and how its structures, commemorating the peaceful meeting of the nations through that great waterway, have fitly been made to represent the art of the entire world, yet with such unity and originality as to give new interest to the ancient forms, and with such a wealth of appropriate symbolism in color, sculpture and mural painting as to make its great courts, towers and arches an inspiring story of Nature's beneficence and Man's progress.

Much of Mr. Macomber's text was written originally for The San Francisco Chronicle, to which acknowledgment is made for its permission to reprint his papers. The popularity of these articles, which have been running since February, has testified to their usefulness. In many cases they have been preserved and passed from hand to hand. They have also won the endorsement of liberal use in other publications. It is proper to say, however, that similarity of language sometimes indicates a common following of the artists' own explanations of their work, made public by the Exposition management.

Mr. Macomber has revised and amplified his chapters hitherto published, and has added others briefly outlining the history of the Exposition, and dealing with the fine-arts, industrial, and livestock exhibits, the foreign and state buildings, music, sports, aviation, and the amusement section. Apart from the smaller guides, the book is thus the first to attempt any comprehensive description of the Exposition. Without indiscriminate praise, or sacrificing independent judgment, the author's purpose has been to interpret and explain the many things about which the visitors on the ground and readers at home may naturally wish to know, rather than to point out minor defects.

For the general exhibit palaces, anything more than a brief outline of their contents would fill several books. But the chapter entitled "The Palace of Fine Arts and its Exhibit, with the Awards," supplies such an account of the plan of the galleries and of the important works therein as will furnish a clear and helpful guide to this great collection. The awards of the Fine Arts juries, just announced, have been incorporated in the account, while a full list of the grand prizes, medals of honor and gold medals also follows the chapter. With the artists thus named are noted the rooms where the works of each may be found. The Appendix offers a practical aid to the study of the "Exposition Art" in the list there given of the mural paintings and sculptures which form the notable decorations of palaces and gardens. With these are cross-references to the pages in the text where they are described.

In selecting the photographs here reproduced, the aim has been not so much to show exhibits as to illustrate the plan, architecture and decorative art of the Exposition, and to indicate the advance which it scores over its predecessors. The pictures, with their full "underlines," will aid those who have not yet visited the Exposition to apprehend its spirit and much of its unprecedented beauty. Cross-references from text to illustrations increase their helpfulness. But even these abundant illustration can do little more than suggest how far the artistic achievement is the finest yet seen in America. No book can adequately represent this World's Fair. Its spell is the charm of color and the grandeur of noble proportion, harmonizing great architectural units; its lesson is the compelling value, demonstrated on a vast scale, of exquisite taste. It must be seen to be understood.

John H. Williams.
San Francisco, July 15, 1915.

I.

Motive and Planning of the Exposition

The Panama Canal a landmark in human progress - Its influence through changes in trade routes San Francisco determines, in spite of the great fire, to celebrate its completion - Millions pledged in two hours - Congressional approval won - The Exposition built by California and San Francisco, without National aid - Only two years given to construction - Fifty millions expended.

Human endeavor has supplied no nobler motive for public rejoicing than the union of the Atlantic and Pacific Oceans. The Panama Canal has stirred and enlarged the imaginations of men as no other task has done, however enormous the conception, however huge the work. The Canal is one of the few achievements which may properly be called epoch-making. Its building is of such signal and far reaching importance that it marks a point in history from which succeeding years and later progress will be counted. It is so variously significant that the future alone can determine the ways in which it will touch and modify the life of mankind.

First of all, of course, its intent is commercial. Experts have already estimated its influence on the traffic routes. But these experts, who can, from known present conditions, work out the changes that will take place, that are already taking place, in the flow of commerce on the seven seas, cannot estimate the effect those changes will have on the life of the people who inhabit their shores. Changes in trade routes have overwhelmed empires and raised up new nations, have nourished civilizations and brought others to decay. From the days when merchants first followed the caravan routes, nothing has so modified the history of nations as the course of the roads by which commerce moved. Huge as was the Canal as a physical undertaking alone, it is not less stupendous in the vision of the effects which will flow from it.

In this vision, the Western shore of the United States feels that it looms largely. No small part of the benefits of the Canal are expected to fall to the Pacific States. Long before it was completed, the minds of men in the West were filled with it. Its approaching completion appealed to everyone as an event of such tremendous significance as to deserve commemoration. Thus when R. B. Hale, in 1904, first proposed that the opening of the waterway should be marked by an international exposition in San Francisco, he merely gave expression to the thought of the whole West.

The Canal is a national undertaking, built by the labor and money of an entire people. It is of international significance, too, for its benefits are world-wide. The Exposition thus represents not only the United States but also the world in its effort to honor this achievement. San Francisco and California have merely staged the spectacle, in which the world participates.

An international exposition is a symbol of world

progress. This one is so complete in its significance, so inclusive of all the best that man has done, that it is something more than a memorial of another event. It is itself epochal, as is the enterprise it commemorates. It bears a direct relation to the Canal. The motive of the Exposition was the grandeur of a great labor. Completed, it embodies that motive in the highest expression of art.

It took eleven years to prepare for and build the Exposition. The first proposal in 1904 was followed by five years of discussion of ways and means. Two years were occupied in raising the money and winning the consent of the Nation, and then four years more in planning, building, and collecting the exhibits. The first plans were interrupted, but not ended, by the most terrible disaster that ever befell a great city - the fire of 1906, which wiped out the entire business portion, with much of the residence section, of San Francisco, and destroyed hundreds of millions of wealth. Before that year ended, and while the city was only beginning its huge task of rebuilding, it again took up its festival idea. A company was formed, but, until reconstruction was largely out of the way, it was impossible to do more than keep the idea alive.

In October, 1909, the idea began to crystallize into a definite purpose. In that month President Taft, at a banquet at the Fairmont Hotel, declared that the Canal would be opened to commerce on January 1, 1915. That announcement gave the final impulse to the growing determination. The success of the Portola celebration that summer had given the city confidence in its ability to carry out a great festival undertaking. In fact, it was at a meeting of the Portola committee that the first move was made toward the organization that later became effective.

A mass-meeting in the Merchants' Exchange, on December 7, 1909, ended in a resolve to organize an exposition company. This found such strong popular support that at a second mass-meeting on April 28, 1910, $4,089,000 was subscribed in less than two hours. In two months the subscription had risen to $6,156,840. Governor Gillett called the California legislature in special session in August to submit to the people constitutional changes enabling San Francisco to issue exposition bonds in the amount of $5,000,000, and the State to raise another $5,000,000 by special tax. In November the people of State and city voted the two amounts. That placed a minimum of $16,000,000 to the credit of the Exposition Company and assured the world that California meant business.

Then followed the struggle for Congressional approval. New Orleans demanded the right to celebrate the opening of the Panama Canal. All the resources of both cities were enlisted in a battle before Congress that drew the attention of the Nation. Three times delegations went from California to Washington to fight for the Exposition. California won, on January 31, 1911, when, by a vote of 188 to 159, the House of Representatives designated San Francisco as the city in which the Panama-Pacific International Exposition should be held in 1915 to commemorate the opening of the Canal.

During this struggle California gave her word that she would not ask the Nation for help in financing the Exposition. The promise has been kept. The Government has not even erected a national building. It has, however, helped in material ways, by granting the use

Ben Macomber

of portions of the Presidio and Fort Mason reservations, by sending naval colliers to bring exhibits from European countries, and by becoming one of the heaviest exhibitors. The national exhibits include three companies of marines encamped on the grounds, and the battleship Oregon anchored off the Marina.

After Congress had acted, half a year was spent in choosing a site. It was at first expected that the Exposition would be built in Golden Gate Park. A compromise among advocates of different sites was reached on July 25, 1911, when a majority vote of the directors named a site including portions of Golden Gate Park, Lincoln Park, the Presidio, and Harbor View. Before 100,000 people President Taft broke ground for the Exposition in the Stadium of Golden Gate Park. But it was not long before the choice settled finally on Harbor View alone.

The work began with the organization of the architectural staff. The following architects accepted places on the commission: McKim, Mead and White, Henry Bacon, and Thomas Hastings of New York; Robert Farquhar of Los Angeles; and Louis Christian Mullgardt, George W. Kelham, Willis Polk, William B. Faville, Clarence R. Ward, and Arthur Brown of San Francisco. To their number was later added Bernard R. Maybeck of San Francisco, who designed the Palace of Fine Arts, while Edward H. Bennett, an associate of Burnham, of Chicago, made the final ground plan of the Exposition group. When San Francisco had been before Congress asking national endorsement for the Exposition here, the plans which were then presented, and on which the fight was won, were prepared by Ernest Coxhead, architect, of this city. These proposed a massed grouping of the

Exposition structures, around courts, and on the Bay front. They were afterwards amplified by Coxhead, and furnished the keynote of the scheme finally carried out. While the Exposition belongs not to California alone, but to the whole world, it is pleasant to find that so much of what is best in it is the work of Californians and San Franciscans.

The architects perfected the plan in 1912. At the same time the actual work of preparing the site was completed with the filling of the tide-land portions by hydraulic dredgers and the removal of the standing buildings. In the same year the department chiefs were named and began their work. John McLaren, for many years Superintendent of Golden Gate Park, was put in charge of the landscape engineering; W. D'A. Ryan was chosen to plan the illumination, and Jules Guerin and K. T. F. Bitter were placed at the heads of the departments of color and sculpture. With these details behind, the ground-breaking for Machinery Palace in January, 1913, marked the beginning of the final stage. In the two years that remained it was necessary only to carry out the plans already perfected. No other exposition has been so forehanded. When the gates opened on February 20, 1915, to remain open till December 4, the Exposition was practically complete. Some of the exhibitors had not finished their installation; some of the foreign nations were not ready, but the Exposition had kept a promise made two years before to have its own work done on time. This achievement was quite unprecedented. It is the more remarkable in that the record was made by a city which had been almost annihilated by fire a few years before.

The entire cost of the Exposition, exclusive of the value of exhibits, is estimated by the Controller at

Ben Macomber

$50,000,000. This total is made up of $20,000,000 spent by San Francisco and California, $10,000,000 laid out in state and foreign buildings and displays, $10,000,000 by private exhibitors, and $10,000,000 by the one hundred concessionaires on the Joy Zone. San Francisco contributed $12,500,000, the State of California $5,000,000, and its fifty-eight counties, $2,500,000. The amounts expended by foreign nations range from $1,700,000 by Argentina to sums as low as $100,000. The State of New York spent nearly $1,000,000.

II.

Ground Plan and Landscape Gardening

The Exposition a product of co-operation of the arts -
The landscape made part of the scheme - Block
grouping of palaces and courts - Plan of the buildings -
McLaren's wonders in gardening - Succession of
flowers throughout the Exposition - Changes overnight - Unique wall of living green.

The artistic quality which distinguishes this Exposition
above all others in America or Europe rests on two
outstanding facts: the substantial unity of its architectural scheme, and its harmony of color, keyed to
Nature's coloring of the landscape in which it is placed.
The site furnished the clue to the plan; co-operation
made possible the great success with which it has been
worked out.

"Centuries ago," said George W. Kelham, chief of
Exposition architecture, "before the modern age of
advanced specialization was dreamed of, had an
architect been asked to create an exposition, he would
have been not only an architect, but painter, sculptor
and landscape engineer as well. He would have
thought, planned and executed from this fourfold
angle, and I doubt if it would have even occurred to
him to think of one of the arts as detached from

Ben Macomber

another." These words express the method of the Exposition builders. The scheme adopted was a unit, in which all of the arts were needed, and in which they all combined to a single end. Each building, each court, every garden and large mass of foliage, was designed as part of a balanced composition. To make the landscape an integral part of the Exposition picture, by fitting the Exposition to the landscape, was the common aim of architect, colorist, sculptor and landscape engineer. The Mediterranean setting offered by a sloping bench on the shore of the Golden Gate suggested, as most capable of high expression of beauty, the scheme of a city of the Far East, its great buildings walled in and sheltering its courts. The coloring of earth, sky and sea furnished the palette from which tints were chosen alike for palaces and gardens.

The beauty of this plan is matched by its practical advantages. The compact grouping of the Exposition palaces not only meant a saving of ground and labor, but it makes it easier to handle the crowds, and lessens the walking required of the visitor. There is no monotony. In developing the general idea, each architect and artist was left free to express his own personality and imagination. The result is that varied forms and colors in the different courts and buildings blend truly into the whole picture of an Oriental city, set in the midst of a vast amphitheater of hills and bay, arched by the fathomless blue of the California sky.

The ground plan is as simple as it is compact. Entering through the main gate at Scott Street, the visitor has the Exposition before him, practically an equal section on either hand. (See map, p. 30, 31.) On right and left in the South Garden are Festival Hall and the Palace of

Horticulture. (p. 23, 24, 29.) In front is the Tower of Jewels, before it the Fountain of Energy. (p. 47.) The tower centers the south front of a solid block of eight palaces, so closely joined in structure, and so harmonized in architecture, as to make really a single palace. On the right and left of the tower are the Palaces of Manufactures and Liberal Arts; beyond them, on east and west, are Varied Industries and Education. Behind these four, and fronting on the bay from east to west, are Mines, Transportation, Agriculture and Food Products. In the center of the group, cut out of the corners of the Manufactures, Liberal Arts, Agriculture and Transportation Palaces, and entered from the south through the Tower of Jewels, is the great Court of the Universe, opened on east and west by the triumphal Arches of the Nations. (p. 59 and 63.) The Court opens northward between the Palaces of Transportation and Agriculture in a splendid colonnaded avenue to the Column of Progress, near the bay. (p. 57.)

Through the arch on the east the Court of the Universe opens into an avenue which leads to the Court of the Ages, cut out of the intersection of the four Palaces of Manufactures, Varied Industries, Mines and Transportation. (p. 70.) A similar avenue on the west passes to the Court of Seasons, carved from the common junction of Liberal Arts, Education, Food Products and Agriculture. (p. 79 and 80.) Avenues pass east and west and to the north from each of these two courts, and on the south each connects through an arch with a court set back into the south front of the palace group, the Courts of Flowers and Palms. (p. 85, 87, 88, 93, 100.) On east and west of this central group of eight palaces are the Palace of Machinery and the Palace of Fine Arts (p. 105, 112), serving architecturally to

Ben Macomber

balance the scheme. East of the exhibit palaces is the Joy Zone, a mile-long street solidly built with bizarre places of amusement. Balancing the Zone on the west is the State and Foreign section, with the live-stock exhibits, the polo field, race track and stadium beyond, at the western extremity of the grounds. The state buildings stand along two avenues on the north side of the section; the foreign pavilions occupy its southern half.

The Tower of Jewels and the central palace group face south on the Avenue of Palms (p. 18), which, at its west end, turns as it passes the Fine Arts lagoon, and becomes the Avenue of Nations. This latter highway, bordered by the foreign buildings, joins at its western extremity the Esplanade, a broad avenue passing the north face of the palace group and continuing westward between the state and the foreign sections.

On the east, the Avenue of Progress divides the central group from the Palace of Machinery. Administration Avenue on the west separates the central group from the Palace of Fine Arts. Along the bay shore is the Marina, and between it and the Esplanade are the Yacht Harbor and the lawns of the North Gardens.

Surrounding all these buildings, filling the courts and bordering the avenues, are John McLaren's lovely gardens. For multitudes of visitors this landscape gardening is the most wonderful thing about the Exposition. The trees and flowers have been placed with perfect art; they look as though they had been there always. It is hard for a stranger to believe that three years ago the Exposition site was a marsh, and that these trees were transplanted last year.

The Avenue of Palms is bordered on each side for half a mile with a double row of California fan palms and Canary date palms, trees from eighteen to twenty-five feet high and festooned higher than a man's head with ivy and blooming nasturtium. (See p. 18.) These massive plants, soil, roots, vines and all, were brought bodily from Golden Gate Park. Against the south walls of the buildings facing this avenue are banked hundreds of eucalyptus globulus, forty to fifty feet high, with smaller varieties of eucalyptus, and yellow flowering acacias.

The Avenue of Progress is bordered with groups of Draceona indivisa, averaging twenty feet in height. The walls of the palaces on either hand are clothed with tall Monterey and Lawson cypresses and arbor vitae. Between these and the Draceonas of the avenue are planted specimens of Abies pinsapo, the Spanish fir. Banks of flowers and vines cover the ground around the bases of the trees. Administration Avenue has on one side the thickets of the Fine Arts lagoon, on the other, masses of eucalyptus globulus against the palace walls, finished off with other hardy trees and shrubs. Against the north front of the palaces are set Monterey cypresses and eucalyptus, banked with acacias.

The entire city side of the South Gardens is bordered by a wondrous wall of living green, - not a hedge, but truly a wall, - the most surprising of all McLaren's inventions. For this wall, though living, is not rooted in the ground, but is really a skeleton of timbers, three times the height of a man, paneled solidly on both sides with shallow boxes of earth thickly set with a tiny green plant, which, as though crushed down by the weight of its name, Mesembryantliemum spectabilis,

Ben Macomber

hugs the soil closely. Each box, really nothing more than a tray, is barely deep enough to contain a couple of inches of earth, and is screened over with wire mesh to prevent the slice of soil from falling out when it is set on edge. Some thousands of these boxes are required to cover the entire wall, which thus appears a solid mass of greenery. The little plant looks like the common ice-plant of old-fashioned gardens, and is actually kin to it. It asks little of this world, is accustomed to grow in difficult places, and is kept green by sprinkling. If a section of it gives up the struggle, the tray may be replaced with a fresh one. From time to time a blush of tiny pink flowers runs over the wall. There seems to be no season for the blossoms, but whenever the sun shines, this delicate shimmer of bloom appears.

The season opened in the great sunken garden of the Court of the Universe with solid masses of rhodo-dendron. The Court of the Ages was a pink flare of hyacinths, which, with an exquisite sense of the desert feeling of the court, were stripped of their leaves and left to stand on bare stalks. The South Gardens and the Court of Flowers were a golden glow of daffodils. Daffodils, too, were everywhere else, with rhododen-dron just breaking into bloom. The daffodil show lasted several weeks until, over night, it was replaced by acres of yellow tulips blooming above thick mats of pansies. This magic change was merely the result of McLaren's forethought. The daffodils had all been set at the right time to bloom when the Exposition opened. The pansies were set with them, but were unnoticed beneath the taller daffodils. Unnoticed also were the tulips, steadily shooting upward to be ready in bloom the moment the daffodils began to fail. One night and morning scores of workmen clipped off all the fading daffodils, and left a yellow sea of tulips with cups just opening. When the tulips faded early, because of continued rains, the solid masses of pansies remained to keep up the golden show. With the end of the yellow period came three months of pink flowers, to be followed in the closing third of the Exposition's life by a show of variegated blooms.

This marvelous sequence of flowers without a gap is not the result of chance, or even of California's floral prodigality, but of McLaren's hard-headed calculation. He actually rehearsed the whole floral scheme of the Exposition for three seasons beforehand. To a day, he knew the time that would elapse between the planting and the blooming of any flower he planned to use. Thus he scheduled his gardening for the whole season so that the gardens should always be in full bloom. In McLaren's program there are ten months of constant bloom, without a break, without a wait. No such gardening was ever seen before. Needless to say, it could hardly have been attempted elsewhere than in California.

Ben Macomber

III.

The South Gardens

A charming foreground to the great palaces - Palace of Horticulture and some of its rare plants - Food for pirates - Ancient and blue-blooded forest dwarfs - The Horticultural Gardens - House of Hoo Hoo - Festival Hall, with its fine sculptures by Sherry Fry - A remarkable pipe organ.

Entering the Exposition by the main or Scott Street gate, the visitor has before him the beautiful South Gardens. (See p. 23.) These form an animated and effective foreground for the Exposition palaces. Except for their fountains, the gardens and the structures in them are less notable for sculpture than the central courts of the Exposition. Most of the plastic work here is purely decorative. The gardens are formal, French in style, laid out with long rectangular pools, each with a formal fountain, and each surrounded by a conventional balustrade with flower receptacles and lamp standards. In harmony with their surroundings, the buildings, too, are French, of florid, festival style.

The Palace of Horticulture, Bakewell and Brown, architects, is the largest and most splendid of the garden structures. (p. 24.) Byzantine in its architecture, suggesting the Mosque of Ahmed I, at Constantinople, its Gallic decorations have made it essentially French in spirit. The ornamentation of this palace is the most florid of any building in the Exposition proper. Yet this opulence is not inappropriate. In size and form, no less than in theme, the structure is well adapted to carry such rich decoration. This is the palace of the bounty of nature; its adornment symbolizes the rich yield of California fields.

In harmony also with the theme, the human figure is absent from the sculpture, save in the caryatids of the porches and the groups supporting the tall finials. Fruits and flowers, interwoven in heavy garlands and overflowing from baskets and urns, carry out the idea of profuse abundance. The great dome, larger than the dome of either St. Peter's at Rome or the Pantheon at Paris, is itself an overturned fruit basket, with a second latticed basket on its top. The conception of profusion becomes almost barbaric in the three pavilioned entrances, flanked on either side by the tall finials suggesting minarets. Here the Oriental influence of the architectural form, the mosque, becomes most pronounced, changing to French again in the caryatid porches.

Altogether, the Palace of Horticulture is a beautiful building, but rather hard to see properly from the ground. From an elevation, where it appears more as a whole, it is far more effective. Curiously, it photographs better than any other building here, save the Fine Arts Palace, but in actual view it hardly lives up to the pictures. Perhaps this is because the comparatively small portions of the structure seen between the trees near-by are dwarfed by the huge dome, while in photographs the camera emphasizes the lower and nearer sections and reduces the proportions

Ben Macomber

of the dome.

The exhibit housed under the great dome should not be passed by. A vivid bit of the tropics is the Cuban display. Here, in an atmosphere artificially heated and moistened to reproduce the steaming jungle, is massed a splendid exhibit of those island trees and flowers that most of us know only through pictures and stories of southern seas. Around the central source of light, which is hidden under tropic vines, stands a circle of royal palms; and planted thickly over the remaining space are jungle trees, vivid enough to our imagination, but many of which have never before been seen in this country.

Boys who feel pirate blood in their veins will revel in this reproduction of the scenes of imagined adventure. Any reasonable pirate could be quite happy here. For here is the breadfruit tree, read of in many a tale of castaways; also the cocoanut palm, with the fruits hanging among the fronds, waiting for the legendary monkey to scamper up the trunk and hurl the great balls at the heads of the beholders. Here, too, are the mango, and many sorts of bananas, and the cabbage palm, another favorite resource of starving adventurers. With these there are other jungle denizens, - the bamboo palm, the paperleaf palm, splendid specimens of the world-old cycad family, the guanabana, and a Tom Thumb palm, which, full grown, is no more than a handbreadth high.

Ancient among trees are the two specimens of microcycas from the swamps of Cuba. These Methuselahs of the forest are at least 1,000 years old, according to the botanists. They are among the slowest growing of living things, and neither of them is much taller than a man. They were seedlings when Alfred the Great ruled England, and perhaps four feet high when Columbus first broke through the western seas. In the four centuries of Cuban history they have not grown so much again.

These venerable trees belong to the bluest-blooded aristocracy of the vegetable world. Ages ago they inhabited our northern states. Their family has come down practically unchanged from the steaming days of the Carboniferous period, when ferns grew one hundred feet high, and thronged with other rank tropical growths in matted masses to form the coal measures. The fossil remains of cycads in the rocks of that period prove that they once flourished in the tropic swamps where now are the hills of Wyoming and Dakota.

Scattered among the trees is a host of flowering vines, of huge crotons with variegated leaves, giant gardenias and tropical lilies. When these bloom, the air of this transplanted jungle is heavy with the perfume of their own island habitat.

The Horticultural Gardens south of the Palace belong to it, and contain a large part of the horticultural exhibits. As they were planted for competitive exhibition purposes, they will not show the constant beauty that appears in the South Gardens. Here we must wait for the flowers in their season, and not expect to have them changed overnight for us by the gardeners' magic.

Back of this horticultural garden is the House of Hoo Hoo, in Forestry Court, flanked by the Pine and Redwood Bungalows. It needs but a glance at its

Ben Macomber

beguiling loveliness to know that here is another lesson in art and architecture by Bernard Maybeck. Here again is poetry in architecture, of a different order from the noble theme of Maybeck's Fine Arts Palace, but none the less poetry. This is a sylvan idyll, telling of lofty trees, cool shades, and secret bowers of fern and vine and wild flower, in the moist and tangled redwood forests. There is little used but rough-barked tree trunks, but what delicate harmony of arrangement!

This lumbermen's lodge is one building outside the Exposition palaces that should not be missed, even though almost hidden away against the south wall. It is worth pondering over. No one may want to build a house like it, but it proclaims how beauty can be attained with simple materials and just proportions.

Festival Hall, Robert Farquhar, architect, balances the Palace of Horticulture in the architectural plan of the South Gardens. (p. 29.) It, too, is French in style, its architecture suggested by the Theatre des Beaux Arts in Paris, a design which furnished the dome necessary to harmonize with that of the palace to the west. As architecture, however, it fails to hold up its end with the splendid Horticultural Palace. Its dome is too large, and has too little structure around it, to be placed so near the ground without an effect of squattiness. Its festive adornment is extremely moderate. On the cornice above the main entrance is the rhyton, the ancient Greek drinking horn, symbol of festivity.

The sculpture, all done by Sherry E. Fry, carries out the same idea. The graceful figures poised on the corner domes are Torch Bearers. On the pylons at either end of the semicircular arcade of the main entrance are two reclining figures. On the right is

Bacchus, with his grapes and wineskin, - a magnificently "pickled" Bacchus! On the left a woman is listening to the strains of festal music. (p. 32.) Each of the pedestals before the false windows at the ends of the arcade supports a figure of Flora with garlands of flowers. On the ground below the two Floras are two of the most delightful pieces of all the Exposition sculpture. One is a little Pan, pipes in hand, sitting on a skin spread over an Ionic capital. This is a real boy, crouching to watch the lizard that has crawled out from beneath the stone. The other is a young girl dreaming the dreams of childhood. There is something essentially girlish about this. Unfortunately, it is now almost hidden by shrubbery.

Within Festival Hall is one of the half-dozen greatest organs in the world. It has more than 7,000 pipes. The heaviest of them weigh as much as 1,200 pounds apiece. Though mere size is not the essential quality of a fine instrument, it is hard to ignore the real immensity of this. The echo organ alone is larger than most pipe organs. This complementary instrument, which is played from the console of the main organ, is placed under the roof of the hall, above the center of the ceiling. Its tones, floating down through the apertures in the dome, echo the themes of the great organ.

Few organs have so mighty a note as the sixty-four-foot open pitch attainable on the Exposition's instrument. Speaking by itself, this note has no sound. It is only a tremendous quaking of the whole building, as though the earth were shuddering. By itself it has no place in organ music. It is not intended to be struck alone. It is used only as a foundation upon which to build other tones. In combination it adds majesty to the music, rumbling in a gigantic undertone to the lighter notes.

Even the open stops in this organ are of more than ordinary dimensions. The usual limit in a pipe organ is the sixteen-foot open stop. But in this organ there are several pipes, both of wood and of metal, thirty-two feet or more in length.

Two small buildings, balanced on either side of the Scott-street entrance, are the Press Building and the Exposition home of the National Young Women's Christian Association. They are alike, French in style, and fronted with caryatid porches.

The real glory of the South Gardens lies in their flowers, and in the charming setting the landscape engineers have here given to the south facade of the palace group. There is the air of Versailles in the planned gayety of the scene. In this the pools and fountains, the formal gardens, the massed trees and shrubbery, and the two palaces themselves, play their part.

IV.

The Walled City: It's Great Palaces and their Architecture, Color and Material

The central group of Exposition structures really a single vast palace, behind a rampart - Historical fitness of such architecture here - The south facade - Spanish portals of Varied Industries and Education Palaces - Italian Renaissance portals of Manufactures and Liberal Arts, and of the Courts of Flowers and Palms - The Roman west wall - Ornate doorway of north facade Interior courts and aisles - A balanced plan - This the first exposition to adopt the colors of nature for its structures - Jules Guerin's color scheme, designed for an artificial travertine marble - Simplicity of his palette, from which he painted the entire Exposition - Even the flowers and sanded walks conform.

Although there are eight buildings named in the central palace group, these are so closely connected in design and structure that in reality they make but one palace. Here is seen the unity with variety which marks this Exposition above all others. Commemorating a great international event, its architecture is purposely eclectic, cosmopolitan. Under a dominating Moorish-Spanish general form, the single architect of the group, W. B. Faville, of San Francisco, drawing upon the

Ben Macomber

famous styles of many lands and schools, has combined into an ordered and vastly impressive whole not only the structural art of Orient and of the great Spanish builders, but also the principles of the Italian Renaissance and the architecture of Greece and Rome from which it sprang. Thus the group is wholly Southern in its origin. There is no suggestion here of the colder Gothic architecture of the North.

Differing from each other in many details, the eight palaces are alike in their outer walls, their domes and gables, and similar in their entrances. These portals give a distinctive character to each palace. While the palaces differ widely in details of decoration, they all have a common source; they are all Mediterranean, - not all Byzantine, or Roman, or Italian, or Spanish, or Moorish, but some thing of each. The manner in which these forms are carried over from one palace to another, and the almost constant recurrence of some of them, like the Moorish domes at the corners, blends them without jar or break. The great wall, almost blank, except for the entrances, encloses the palaces like a walled city of the Mediterranean or the nearer Orient. Such a walled city it is, with its courts, its avenues, its fountains and pools, all placed in a setting of landscape, sea and sky, that might belong to Spain, or Southern Italy, or the lands of the Moslem.

The broad, unbroken spaces that mark each face of this vast block greatly heighten the illusion. They lend an Old-World aspect, the historical fitness of which must not be overlooked. For these plain surfaces are indeed significant in the celebration of an event which was predicted by the Spanish conquistadors a century before the English Cavaliers and Puritans laid the foundations of our American Commonwealth.

Relieved only by the foliage that is finely massed against them, the great blank spaces of the "Walled City" recall the severer side of Mediterranean architecture, just as their gorgeously ornate portals, towers and domes speak of its warmth and color. They are an architectural feature that has traveled far. The unbroken rampart, born of the need of defense in immemorial cities on the east and south shores of the Mediterranean, was carried thence by the Moors to Spain, to go in turn with the conquerors of the New World, and became a characteristic of the civic and ecclesiastical architecture of Latin America. Hence it is not without meaning and reason that this historic architectural form, the blank exterior of the walled city, has found its finest use in the far-western city of St. Francis. Quite apart from their frequent occurrence in the mission architecture of old Alta California, these simple wall spaces well befit the monumental structure that honors an achievement so important to all Spanish America as the Panama Canal.

The southern front of the group, facing the Avenue of Palms, has the aspect of a single palace, opened in the center by the noble Roman arch of the Tower of Jewels, and indented by the Court of Flowers and the Court of Palms. (See p. 18, 88.) Seen across the South Gardens, the whole facade rising from the trees along the wall, is wondrously beautiful. The wall is seventy feet high, topped with a red-tiled roof. The pale green domes over the centers of the palaces are Byzantine, a style much used in the mosques of Islam. The gables are each crowned with a figure of Victory, sometimes called an "acroterium," from the architectural name of the tablet on which it stands. The towers on either side of the entrances to the courts are Italian. The little towers buttressing the domes on the corners of the

Ben Macomber

palaces at the extreme right and left of the front, and from there repeated around the east, west and north walls, are Moorish, with characteristic latticed windows.

The Palace of Varied Industries, on the extreme right, is made entirely Spanish in its southern front by its beautiful central portal, modeled after the sixteenth-century entrance to the Hospice of Santa Cruz at Toledo. (pp. 18, 37.) Except for the sculpture, in which the Spanish saints have been replaced by figures of industry, the portal is a copy of the original. All the figures are the work of Ralph Stackpole, whose treatment of the subjects, no less than their exalted position in the niches of the saints, has dignified the workman.

On each side of the entrance is the "Man with a Pick." The group in the tympanum represents Varied Industries. (p. 138.) The central figure is Agriculture, the basic food-supplying industry. On one side is the Builder, on the other the Common Workman. Beyond them are Commerce holding the figurehead of a ship, and a woman with a spindle, a lamb before her, typifying the textile industries.

The figure in the keystone represents the Power of Industry. Under the upper canopy is an old man handing his burden to a younger one, the Old World passing its burdens on to the New World. The infant figures come from the Spanish original.

The two lesser portals on the south side of this palace are likewise Spanish. In the grill work of their openings, designed in imitation of metal, as well as in that of the central portal, there is a strong suggestion of the Arabian architecture brought into Spain by the Moors. Indeed, there is something Moorish about the whole work, except that the Mohammedans do not represent living things in art. A passage in the Koran tells devout followers of the prophet that if they should carve or picture a plant or animal they would be called upon at the Judgment to make it real. Sometimes, however, they employed Christian workmen to execute such representations, being quite resigned to let the unbeliever risk damnation.

The bears terminating the buttresses on the walls represent California, and hold the seal of the State. Such buttresses against a plain wall, with a tiled roof, are common in the Franciscan missions of California.

The Palaces of Manufactures and Liberal Arts, on either side of the Tower of Jewels, are alike on the south, and Italian. The Moorish corner domes are omitted here, as the palaces terminate on one side in one of the Italian towers and on the other in the wings of the Tower of Jewels. The central portals are Italian, with tiled roofs and latticed grills, with handsome imitations of bronze work under the arches. The friezes over the arches as well as the figures in the niches are by Mahonri Young, of New York. The frieze represents industries of various kinds, the work of women as well as of men. In the niche on the left is a woman with a spindle, on the right a workman with a sledgehammer. Like Stackpole's figures on the portal of Varied Industries, Young's sculptures are simple and strong. The lion used as the keystone figure of the arch and the lions and elephants alternating as fountain heads in the niches in the wall give an Oriental touch to these palaces.

Ben Macomber

Of their portals none are more beautiful than those leading from the Courts of Flowers and Palms. All four are finely expressive of the noblest architecture of the Italian Renaissance. They glow with the sunshine and color of Italy. Those entering the Palaces of Liberal Arts and Education from the Court of Palms are identical in design, and seem almost perfect in their harmonious lines and warm color. (p. 88.) The other pair, opening from the Palaces of Manufactures and Varied Industries into the Court of Flowers, are cheery portals, made more domestic in feeling by the loggia between the colonnade and the tiled roof. (p. 85, 100.)

The three portals of the Palace of Education are of the Spanish Renaissance, and the Moorish towers reappear at the corners. The twisted columns of the entrances are Byzantine. The tympanum above the central portal contains Gustav Gerlach's group "Education." (p. 138.) In the center is the teacher with her pupils, seated under the Tree of Knowledge; on the left, the mother instructs her children; on the right, the young man, his school days past, is working out for himself a problem of science. Thus the group pictures the various stages of education, from its beginning at home to that training in the school of life which ends only at death. The cartouche just above the entrance bears the Book of Knowledge, shedding light in all directions, the curtains of darkness drawn back by the figures at the side. The hour glass below the book counsels the diligent use of time; the crown above symbolizes the reward of knowledge. The banded globe over the portal signifies that education encompasses the world.

Above each of the flanking portals is an inset panel representing the Teacher, a woman at the left, a man at the right. The man looks toward the woman, thus signifying that the world is no longer dependent on man alone.

Turning the corner, the entire west wall of the palaces becomes Roman to accord with the Roman Palace of Fine Arts across the lagoon. The characteristic features are the Roman half-domes above the entrances, and the sculptures repeated in the niches of the walls. (p. 119.) On this side, the Palaces of Education and Food Products are alike, except for a slight difference in the vestibule statuary and the fountains.

On the great Sienna columns beside the half-domes stands Ralph Stackpole's "Thought." The semicircle of female figures in the vestibule of the dome of the Palace of Education, bearing in their hands books with the motto "Ex Libris," though the preposition is omitted, represents the store of knowledge in books. The similar array of men bearing wreaths of cereals in the half-dome of the Palace of Food Products signifies the source of vigor in the fruits of the soil. The simple Italian fountains in the vestibules, the work of W. B. Faville, are decorative and beautiful.

The alternated groups in the niches along the wall are "The Triumph of the Fields" and "Abundance." This is well called archaeological sculpture, for the emblems are from the dim past, and can be understood only with the help of an archaeological encyclopaedia. In the first are the bull standard and the Celtic cross, which were carried through the fields in ancient harvest festivals. In the second, the objects heaped around the lady suggest abundance.

The north facade of the palace group is an unbroken Spanish wall, blank, except for the four beautiful and

Ben Macomber

identical sixteenth-century portals. (See p. 43.) This magnificent decoration, suggestive of the finest work in rare metals, is, in fact, called "plateresque," from its resemblance to the work of silversmiths. The figures looking out on the blue water that reaches to Panama and the shores of Peru, are historical. In the center is the Conquistador. Flanking his stately figure on each side is the pirate of the Spanish Main, the adventurer who served with but a color of lawful war under Drake, the buccaneer that followed Morgan to the sack of Panama. (p. 44.) These statues are by Allen Newman.

Every man jack of the eight pirates on the four portals is apparently bow-legged. There is a vast space between the knees of these buccaneers of Panama, but when you look more closely it is hard to decide whether those pirate knees are really sprung, or whether it is the posture of the figures that suggests the old quip about the pig in the alley. The sculptor has at least given to the figures a curious effect of bandy legs. The feet are set wide apart, the space between and behind the legs is deeply hollowed out, and the rope which hangs from the hands curves in over the feet to add to the illusion. There used to be a saying that cross-eyed people could not be honest. Similarly, perhaps, Newman thought the appearance of bow-legs would increase the villainy of his pirate. Certainly, no such blood-curdling ruffian has been seen out of comic opera.

The east wall of the palace group becomes Old Italian, to harmonize with the Roman architecture of the Machinery Palace opposite. The portals suggest those of ancient Italian city walls. In the niches stands Albert Weinert's "Miner, " here used because the Palace of

Mines forms one half the wall.

In the long avenue that runs east and west through the center of the group, the unity of the eight buildings becomes more apparent as we view the noble arches which join them, and note the character of their inner facades. Education and Food Products are alike in the walls and portals fronting on the dividing aisle. The Spanish architecture of the south facade of Education is here carried over to Food Products. Similarly, the avenue between Mines and Varied Industries is the same on both sides, carrying out the Old Italian of the east front, and with The Miner repeated in the portal niches of both palaces. The avenues leading from the Court of the Universe to the Court of Ages and the Court of Seasons have been variously called the Aisles of the Rising and the Setting Sun, or the Venetian and Florentine Aisles. Their four walls are in the style of the Italian Renaissance, and show a diaper design similar to that on the Italian towers of the Courts of Flowers and Palms.

In an artistic sense, this group is incomplete without the Palace of Fine Arts on the west and Machinery Hall on the east. (p. 105, 106.) Balancing each other in the general scheme, they form the necessary terminals of the axis of the Exposition plan. This matter of balance has been carefully thought out everywhere, and affords a fine example of the co-operation of the many architects who worked out the vast general design. The Courts of Seasons and Ages are set off against each other; the Courts of Palms and Flowers weigh equally one against the other; the Arches of the Nations not only balance but match; even the Tower of Jewels, which is the center of the whole plan, is offset by the Column of Progress. In the South Gardens, the

Ben Macomber

Palace of Horticulture is balanced against Festival Hall.

Color and Material. - All other Expositions have been almost colorless. This is the first to make use of the natural colors of sea and sky, of hill and tree, and to lay upon all its grounds and buildings tints that harmonize with these. Jules Guerin, the master colorist, was the artist who used the Exposition as a canvas on which to spread glorious hues. Guerin decided, first, that the basic material of the buildings should be an imitation of the travertine of ancient Roman palaces. On this delicate old ivory background he laid a simple series of warm, yet quiet, Oriental hues, which, in their adaptation to the material of construction and to the architecture, as well as in their exquisite harmony with the natural setting, breeds a vast respect for his art.

The color scheme covers everything, from the domes of the buildings down to the sand in the driveways and the uniforms of the Exposition guards. The walls, the flags and pennants that wave over the buildings, the shields and other emblems of heraldry that hide the sources of light, draw their hues from Guerin's plan. The flowers of the garden conform to it, the statuary is tinted in accordance with it, and even the painters whose mural pictures adorn the courts and arches and the Fine Arts Rotunda were obliged to use his color series. The result gives such life and beauty and individuality to this Exposition as no other ever had. It makes possible such beautiful ornamentation as the splendid Nubian columns of the Palace of Fine Arts, and the glories of the arches of the Court of the Universe. (See frontispiece.)

Go into that Court on a bright day and take note of the art that has made Nature herself a part of the color plan. From a central position in the court, where one can look down the broad approach leading from the bay, Nature spreads before the beholder two expanses of color, the deep blue of salt water sparkling in the sun, and the not less deep, but more ethereal, blue of the California sky. With this are the browns and greens of the hills beyond the bay, and, nearer at hand, the vivid verdure of lawns and trees and shrubs. All these the designer used as though they were colors from his own palette. To go with them in his scheme he chose for pillar and portico, for the wall spaces behind, for arch and dome, for the decorations and for material of the sculptures, such hues that the whole splendid court and its vistas of palaces beyond blend with the colors of sea and sky and of green living things in a glorious harmony.

Such a view of the heart of the Exposition at its best compels recognition of Guerin's skill in color. It needed a vivid imagination to realize the possibilities of the scene, and visualize it. It required infinite delicacy and a fine sense of the absolute rightness of shade and tint to produce such harmonious beauty. The mere thought of it is a lesson in art.

The decision of the architects to develop the theme of an Oriental walled city, and the natural setting of the site, Mediterranean in its sea and sky, led Guerin to select Oriental colors. Aiming at simplicity, he decreed that not more than eight or nine colors should be found upon the subdued palette from which he would paint the Exposition. Then he took into consideration the climate and atmospheric conditions peculiar to San Francisco. Every phase of sky and sea and land, every

Ben Macomber

shadow upon the Marin hills, across the bay, was noted in choosing an imitation of natural travertine for the key color of the Palaces.

This is a pale pinkish-gray-buff, which may be called old ivory. It is not garish, as a dead white would be, especially in the strong California sunlight, but soft and restful to the eye. It harmonizes with the other colors selected, and, most important of all, it avoids a certain "new" effect which pure white would give, and which is deadly to art.

Paul Deniville, who had already developed a successful imitation of travertine, was engaged to make the composition to be applied over the exterior walls. This is a reproduction in stucco of the travertine marble of the Roman palaces of the period of Augustus. This marble is a calcareous formation deposited from the waters of hot springs, usually in volcanic regions, and is common in the hills about Rome. It often contains the moulds left by leaves and other materials incorporated in the deposit. These account for the corrugations of the stone when it is cut. In California, as in other regions where hot springs are found, travertine is not uncommon. It is found notably in the volcanic district of Mono County, and elsewhere, sometimes in the form of Mexican onyx, which is only a translucent variety of the same marble. In its reproduction here the marble has been imitated even to the natural imperfections which roughened the Italian stone. In the concave surfaces of the ornamentation the color has been deepened, so that it appears sometimes as a rich reddish brown. All this enhances the antique effect, making the palace walls and columns still more like those of the old Roman construction.

Besides the travertine the eight other colors employed are:

1. French Green, used in all lattices, flower tubs, curbing of great plats, where it complements the green of the grass, In the exterior woodwork and some of the smaller doors.

2. Oxidized Copper Green, a peculiar mottled light green. All the domes, except the six yellow ones in the Court of the Universe, are of this light green. It forms a sharp contrast with the blue sky and a pleasing topping to the travertine walls.

3. Blue Green, found in the ornamentation of the travertine, and in the darker shades at the bases of the flag poles. These first three colors, all in tones of green, are regarded as one unit in the spectrum of nine colors allowed by Guerin.

4. Pinkish-Red-Gold, used in the flag poles and lighting standards only. It is a very brilliant and striking pigment, and is always topped with gold.

5. Wall-Red, used in three tones. They are found in the backgrounds of the colonnades, courts and niches, on the tiled roofs, and in the statuary. These reds run from terra-cotta to a deep russet, and predominate in the interiors of the principal courts.

6. Yellow-Golden-Orange, largely used in enriching the travertine and in enhancing shadow effects. It is found in the architectural mouldings and in much of the statuary. The following rule was adopted in regard to the coloring of the statuary: That which is high off the ground, that is, the figures surmounting the domes

Ben Macomber

and spires, is of golden yellow, while that close to the eye of the beholder is of verde-antique, a rich copper-green streaked with gray, and much is left in the natural travertine tint.

7. Deep Cerulean Blue and Oriental Blue, verging upon green, are used in the ceilings and other vaulted recesses, in deep shadows, in coffers and in the background or ornamentation in which travertine rosettes are set in cerulean blue panels. It might be called electric blue. It is brilliant and at the same time in harmony with the other colors.

8. Gray, very similar to the travertine.

9. Marble Tint, spread over the travertine in places with a transparent glaze.

10. Verde-Antique, really one of the many shades of green - a combination of the copper-green and a soft gray, and therefore not to be counted as one of the nine cardinal colors. It simulates corroded copper, and has faint yellow and black lines.

With the gamut thus restricted by the taste and discrimination of a master, the decorators and artists were strictly limited to the nine colors named. No one might use other than cerulean blue, if he employed blue at all; no other red than the tone popularly known as "Pompeiian" has been admitted in the scheme. In this red the admixture of brown and yellow nullify any tendency towards carmine on crimson. The French and the copper greens and the intermediate shades approved by Guerin are the only greens allowed.

Here is seen the great advantage of a one-man idea. No

other exposition was ever so carefully or successfully planned in this particular. There is no court of one color clashing with a dome, palace or tower of conflicting tone, whether near by or at a distance. All is in harmony.

Working with Guerin, John McLaren, in charge of the landscape gardening, so selected the flowers which border the paths and fill the parterres that they too conform to the color scheme. Though three different complete floral suits are to be seen at the Exposition in three periods, each one accords with the hues of wall and tower, completing in harmony the effect of the whole. The pinkish sand spread on the paths and avenues to harmonize with other ground colors was not always tinted. Some one had noticed that the white beach sand at Santa Cruz turned pink when heated. Seizing upon this fact, McLaren and Guerin used it to give a final touch to their scheme of color. They drew another lesson from the washerwoman. A familiar laundry device was used to give sparkle and brilliance to the waters of the pools and lagoons. They were blued, not by dumping indigo into the water, but by tinting the bottoms with blue paint.

Ben Macomber

V.

The Tower of Jewels

Imposing as the central accent of the Exposition's architecture - Its magic glow at night - A magnificent Roman arch - "Jewels" of the Tower - An historical landmark - Inscriptions, sculpture and murals - Fountains of "Youth" and "El Dorado" - An epitome of the Exposition's art.

The Tower of Jewels, Carrere and Hastings, architects, is the central structure in the Exposition architecture. (See p. 47.) It plays a triple role. In architecture it is the center on which all the other buildings are balanced. In relation to the theme of the Exposition, it is the triumphal gateway to the commemorative celebration of an event the history of which it summarizes in its sculpture, painting and inscription. Last of all, it is an epitome of the Exposition art.

Towering above everything else, it is at once the culminating point and the center of the Exposition scheme. It links the palaces of the central group, otherwise divided into two sections. Upon it rests the balance of Festival Hall and the Palace of Horticulture, of the courts, the gardens, the Palace of Machinery and the Palace of Fine Arts. It finds its own balancing structure in the Column of Progress. It is intended to be the first thing seen from afar, the point from which the eye travels to lesser things on either hand.

At night the Tower remains the center of the transformed Exposition. Under the white light of the powerful projectors, details disappear, the structure is softened into a form almost ghostly. It becomes ethereal. All its daytime glitter gone, it seems really spiritual. The jewels hung over the upper portion do not flash out a diamond brilliance, as they might have been expected to do; rather they spread the light in a soft film about the Tower. (p. 135.)

From close at hand, the arch and its flanking colonnades are truly imperial. There the ornamentation and color of the upper part are not in the eye. Up to the cornice above the arch, the mass of the Tower is magnificent in proportion and harmonious in line and color. It almost seems that the builders might have stopped there, or perhaps have finished the massive block of the arch with a triumphant mass of sculpture.

Studied from the ground underneath the Tower and around it, the arch and the two little colonnaded courts in the wings are gloriously free and spacious, with the spaciousness that the Exposition as a whole reflects, that of the sea and sky of its setting. I walked here when the ocean breeze, fresh from winter storms at sea, was sweeping through them. There is no confinement, no sense of imprisonment from the boundless depths of air outside. Something which the architect could not include in his plans has come in to make constant this increase in the sense of freedom and space. The openings of the arches, being the only free and unconfined passageways through the south facade of the palace group, provide the natural draft on

Ben Macomber

this side for the interior courts. The air rushes through at all times, even when no breeze is stirring outside. This uncramped movement of air currents, far from being unpleasant, gives the same sense of open freedom that one gets on a bold headland, where the ocean winds whip the flowers and lay the grass flat.

From the court behind the Tower you see the mansioned hills of San Francisco through the colonnades like panelled strips of painting; and, looking northward, the long spaces over the bay to the great Marin hills beyond.

The jewels on the Tower give it a singularly gay and lively touch when the sun is bright and the wind blowing. The wind is seldom absent around the top of so lofty a structure, and there these bits of glass are always sparkling. At night they produce, under the strong white light of a whole battery of giant reflectors hidden on other buildings, the mystic haze that shrouds the Tower. They were a fine idea of the chief of illumination, W. D'A. Ryan, giving just a touch of brilliance to an Exposition otherwise clothed in soft tones. The jewels are only hard glass, fifty thousand of them cut in Austria for the purpose, prismatic in form, and each backed with a tiny mirror. Hung free to swing in the wind, they sparkle and dance as they catch the sun from different angles.

As the great gate to the Exposition, the Tower becomes historical in relation to the event celebrated beyond its archway. Its purpose, from this point of view, is to tell the entering visitor briefly of the milestones along the way of time up to the digging of the Canal. Its enrichment of sculpture, painting and inscription summarizes the story of Panama and of the Pacific shore northward from the Isthmus. The architect has expressed in its upper decorations something of the feeling of Aztec art. The four inscriptions on the south faces of the arches tell how Rodrigo de Bastides discovered Panama in 1501; how Balboa first saw the Pacific Ocean in 1513; how the United States began to dig the Canal in 1904, and opened it in 1915. The four on the north faces epitomize the history of California, thus honored as the state that commemorates the opening of the Canal. They speak of Cabrillo's discovery of California in 1542, of the founding of the Mission of San Francisco by Moraga, in 1776, of the acquisition of California by the United States, 1846, and its admission to the Union in 1850.

The sculpture carries out the same idea. Pizarro and Cortez sit their horses before the Tower, splendid figures of the Spanish conquerors, the one by Charles C. Rumsey, the other by Charles Niehaus. (p. 48.) Above the entablature of the supporting columns are repeated around the outer wall of the arch, Adventurer and Priest, Philosopher and Soldier, types of the men who won the Americas, all done by John Flanagan. Above the cornice, the mounted figures by F. M. L. Tonetti are those of the Spanish cavaliers, with bannered cross. The eagles stand for the Nation that built the Canal. Excellent in spirit are Flanagan's figures of the four types, especially that of the strikingly ascetic Priest. (p. 44.) Besides their symbolism, the statues fulfill a useful architectural purpose in relieving what would otherwise be the blankness of the wall. But the same cannot be as truly said of the Armoured Horsemen above. Vigorous as they are, they are not in the right place. They clutter up the terrace on which they stand. The globe on the pinnacle, with its band, signifies that now a girdle has

Ben Macomber

been put around the earth.

On the side walls of the arch under the Tower, the murals by William de Leftwich Dodge tell the story of the triumphant achievement which the Exposition commemorates. On the east, the central panel pictures Neptune and his attendant mermaid leading the fleets of the world through the Gateway of All Nations. (p. 53.) On one side Labor, with its machines, draws back from the completed task, and, on the other, the Intelligence that conceived the work and the Science that made it possible, move upward and onward, while a victorious trumpeter announces the triumph. One figure, with covered face, flees from the appeal of the siren, but whom he represents, or why he flees, I cannot tell.

In the smaller panel to the left, Labor is crowned and all who served with toil are acclaimed. Its companion picture on the right represents Achievement. The Mind that conceived the work is throned, the Sciences stand at one side, while a figure crouching before the bearer of rewards points to Labor as equally worthy.

On the west side of the arch, the central panel portrays the meeting of Atlantic and Pacific, with Labor joining the hands of the nations of east and west. In the panel to the left, enlightened Europe discovers the new land, with the savage sitting on the ruins of a forgotten civilization, the Aztec once more. On the right America, with her workmen ready to pick up their tools and begin, buys the Canal from France, whose labor has been baffled.

The two lovely fountains in the wings of the Tower draw their inspiration from the days of the conquistadors. Mrs. Harry Payne Whitney's Fountain of El Dorado is a dramatic representation of the Aztec myth of The Gilded One, which the followers of Cortez, in their greed for gold, mistook for a fact instead of a fable. (p. 54.) The Fountain of Youth by Edith Woodman Burroughs finds its justification as a part of the historical significance of the Tower in the legend of that Fountain of Eternal Youth sought by Ponce de Leon. (p. 53.) The interpretation of these sculptures is set forth in the chapter on Fountains.

The Tower of Jewels epitomizes the Exposition's art. The glories of its architecture, color, sculpture, painting, and landscape gardening all find an expression here. In architecture it reflects something of almost all of the orders found in the Exposition. In the main it is Italian Renaissance, which means that the basic characters are Roman and Greek, enriched with borrowings from the Orient and Byzantium. In column and capital, in wall and arch and vaulted ceiling, it represents the architecture of the whole Exposition, and so harmoniously as to form a singular testimony to the unity of the palace scheme.

In color, from the dull soft gold of the columns of the colonnades on either wing, through the vivid hues of Dodge's allegorical murals under the arch, and the golden orange and deep cerulean blue in the vaulted recesses, up to the striking green of columns on the upper rounds of the Tower, the structure summarizes all the pigments which the master of color, Guerin, has laid upon the Exposition.

In sculpture, the conquistadors in front, the hooded Franciscans and the Spanish warriors who stand around the cornice, the corner figures on the Tower

Ben Macomber

above, and, finally, the great globe on top, repeat in varied form the themes of palace, court, facade, and entrance. It has its own fountains in its own little courts.

Then, as a final touch to complete this epitome of Exposition art, the dark cypresses set in the niches on either side of the openings of the arch, gracefully express the debt the whole palace scheme owes to its landscape engineer. In the original models of the Tower, these niches were designed for vases. It was a happy thought that placed the cypresses there instead.

VI.

The Court of the Universe

Most important of the three great courts of the "Walled City" - A meeting-place of East and West - Roman in its architecture and atmosphere, suggesting the vast Piazza of St. Peter's Triumphal Arches of the Nations - Their types of the great races of Orient and Occident - Fine mural paintings by Simmons and Du Mond - Fountains of the Rising and the Setting Sun - Aitken's "Elements" - The "Column of Progress."

The court is the key to the scheme of the palace group of the Exposition. Leaving out the state and foreign quarters, and the other suburbs, and omitting the Fine Arts Palace and Machinery Hall, which, from a purely architectural standpoint, are merely balanced orna-ments needed to complete the whole, the Exposition city is a palace of blank walls enclosing three superb courts.

The court is an essential element of the Oriental architecture of the Mediterranean, which provided the theme of the Exposition plan. There, however, it is the patio, the place of the siesta, the playground of the children. Here the courts have been made the chief architectural feature of the group. There the courts are private. Here they are merely hidden.

Ben Macomber

The central court at the Exposition, the largest and the most splendid, is the Court of the Universe. (See p. 63.) It is the most important, too, in the story which its sculptures tell, and in its relation to the purpose of the Exposition. Whether it is also the most beautiful is a matter about which opinions differ. Many persons admire Mullgardt's romantic Court of Ages beyond anything else, while others are in love with the calm Court of Seasons. Paradoxically, the Court of the Universe suffers from its very magnificence. It is so vast that the beholder is slow to feel an intimate relation with it. The same is true of some of the noblest sights in nature. First seen, there is something disappointing in the Grand Canyon. There is too much in the view to be comprehended until after many days. In this court, the visitor is pleased with its splendid proportions, its noble arches, its rich sculpture, the wonderful blending of its colors with those of sea and sky; but the pleasure at first is of the intellect rather than of the emotions. Like other big and really fine things, it grows on one. The sweep of its colonnades is majestic, the arches are noble monuments, the Column of Progress is inspiring, the fountains show a graceful play of water, the sculpture is big, strong, and significant; the flowers of the sunken garden are a glory long to be remembered.

The Court of the Universe is Roman in architecture, treated in the style of the Italian Renaissance. Its commanding features, the Triumphal Arches and the magnificent flanking colonnades are most Roman in spirit, their Italian decoration appearing in the medallions and spandrels of the arches, the garlands hung along the entablature of the colonnade, and the interior adornment of the vaulted corridors. The columns, including the huge Sienna shafts before the arches and the Tower of Jewels, are Roman Corinthian, with opulent capitals, though not too florid when used in a work of such vast extent. Most Roman of all is the great Column of Progress, at the north end of the court.

McKim, Mead and White of New York, the architects, had the Piazza of St. Peter's at Rome in mind when they designed this great sweep of colonnades. There, too, they borrowed from the circle of saints the idea of the repeated Star figure. The colonnade not only encloses the court but is produced along the sides of the Palaces of Agriculture and Transportation to form two corridors of almost Egyptian vastness. These two features, the arches and the colonnades, here at the center of the palace group, strike the Exposition's note of breadth. Their decoration is the key to the festal richness of all the adornment.

By day the four entrances to the court are its finest features. Nowhere in the whole Exposition is the air more gloriously free than around the lofty arch and colonnades of the Tower of Jewels. Nowhere is the sunlight purer, or the sky bluer, than over the broad approach leading up from the glancing waters of the bay, past the aspiring Column of Progress, and between the noble colonnades of the palaces on either hand. From within the court, or from the approaches on east and west, the triumphal Arches of the Nations impress one with the magnificence of their proportions, their decoration, and their color. There the Oriental hues of the Exposition are carried upward, to meet and blend with the sky, and magically to make the heavens above them bluer than they really are. (See frontispiece.)

Ben Macomber

There is little Oriental about the court, except the color and the group of the Nations of the East above the Arch of the Rising Sun. The colonnade is Corinthian, all the arches are Roman, the sculpture is classic, the paintings are romantic, mystic, - the Court of the Universe may properly hold all things. It is thus an arena for the expression of universal themes, on which the nations of the East and West look down from their lofty Arches of Triumph. With this key, the symbolism of the sculpture in the court is easy. The Stars, by Calder, stand in circle above the colonnade. The frieze below the cornices of the pavilion towers represents the Signs of the Zodiac, by Herman A. MacNeil.

The graceful figures atop the two fountain columns in the oval sunken garden are the Rising and the Setting Sun, by Adolph A. Weinmann. (p. 69.) In the east the Sun, in the strength of morning, the masculine spirit of "going forth," has spread his wings for flight; in the west, the luminary, now essentially feminine, as the brooding spirit of evening, is just alighting. The sculptural adornment of the shafts is detailed in the chapter on Fountains.

The titanic Elements slumber on the balustrade, one on either hand of the stairways leading down on north and south into the sunken area. (p. 64.) On one side, on the north, the Elemental Power holds in check the Dragon of Fire. The whole figure expresses the primitive terror of Fire, a fear that still lives in the beasts. On the other side lies Water, the roaring Ocean, kelp in his hair, Neptune's trident in his hand, by him one of his fabled monsters. On the south, eagles of the Air hover close to the winged figure of the woman, who holds up the evening star and breathes gently down upon her people. Icarus, who was the first airman, appears upon her wings. Opposite, rests Earth, unconscious that her sons struggle with her. These remarkably expressive figures are the work of Robert Aitken.

The youthful groups by Paul Manship upon the extremities of the balustrade, on either hand of the eastern and western stairways, represent Music and Poetry, Music by the dance, Poetry by the written scroll. The sculpture is archaic in type, - an imitation of Greek imitations of still earlier models.

The colossal groups on the Arches of the Nations symbolize the meeting of the peoples of the East and West, brought together by the Panama Canal, and here uniting to celebrate its completion. In the group of the Nations of the East the elephant bears the Indian prince, and within the howdah, the Spirit of the East, mystic and hidden. (p. 63.) On the right is the Buddhist lama from Tibet, representative of that third of the human race which finds hope of Nirvana in countless repetitions of the sacred formula, "Om Mani Padme Hum." Next is the Mohammedan, with the crescent of Islam; then a negro slave, and then a Mongolian warrior, the ancient inhabitant of the sandy waste, a type of those Tartar hordes which swept Asia under Tamerlane and Genghis Khan. On the left of the Indian elephant are an Arab falconer, an Egyptian mounted on a camel and bearing a Moslem standard, then a negro slave bearing a basket of fruit on his head, and a sheik from the deserts of Arabia, all representing the Mohammedans of the nearer East. Thus are figured types of the great Oriental races, the Hindoo, the Tartar, which includes the Turk and the northern Chinese; the Chinese stock of the south, the Arab, and the Egyptian. Only the Persian is omitted, and possibly the Japanese, unless that, too, is Mongol.

Ben Macomber

On the Arch of the Setting Sun, the prairie schooner is the center of the group of the Nations of the West, on the top a figure of Enterprise, the Spirit of the West. (p. 59.) On either side of her is a boy. These are the Heroes of Tomorrow. Between the oxen rides the Mother of Tomorrow. Beside the ox at the right is the Italian immigrant, behind him the Anglo-American, then the squaw with her papoose, and the horse Indian of the plains. By the ox at the left is the Teuton pioneer, behind him the Spanish conquistador, next, the woods Indian of Alaska, and lastly the French Canadian.

Three sculptors collaborated in the modeling of these groups, A. Stirling Calder, Leo Lentelli, and Frederick G. R. Roth.

Of the Mural Paintings under the Arches of the Nations, the two by Edward Simmons in the arch on the east are an allegory of the movement of the peoples across the Atlantic, while those by Frank Vincent Du Mond in the western arch picture in realistic figures the westward march of civilization to the Pacific. Historically, the picture on the southern wall of the Arch of the Nations of the East comes first. Here Simmons has represented the westward movement from the Old World through natural emigration war, conquest, commerce and religion, personifying these in types of the people who have crossed the Atlantic. On the strand, beyond which appear types of the navies of the ages, are the following: an inhabitant of the fabled Atlantis, here conceived as a savage; the Greek warrior, perhaps one of those who fared with Ulysses over the sea to the west; the adventurer and explorer, portrayed as Columbus; the colonist, Sir Walter Raleigh; the missionary, in garb of a priest; the artist, and the artisan. All are called onward by the trumpet of the Spirit of Adventure, to found new families and new nations, symbolized by the vision of heraldic shields. Behind them stands a veiled figure, the Future listening to the Past. The long period in which this movement has been in progress is expressed by the dress of the travellers.

This might be called the Material Movement to the West, for the picture opposite depicts the Ideals of that progress. Hope leads the way, though some of the Hopes, shown as bubbles, were but Illusions. Then follow Adventure, Art, Imagination, Truth, Religion, and the spirits of domestic life. Simmons' work is characterized by grace and delicacy. The pictures are pleasing as form and color alone, but without titles the allegories are too difficult for people unaccustomed to interpreting this kind of art.

Du Mond's two murals in the western arch are easier. They make a continuous story. The first chapter, on the north side, pictures the emigrant train, led by the Spirit of Adventure, leaving for the West, while the second shows the pioneers reaching the shores of the Pacific and welcomed by California. To express the many-sided development of the West, Du Mond has portrayed individuals as the types of the pioneers. Here are Junipero Serra, the priest; Anza, the Spanish captain who first trod the shores of San Francisco Bay; Joseph Le Conte, the scientist; Bret Harte, the author; William Keith, the artist; and Starr King, the divine. The energy of these men has actually outstripped the Spirit of Adventure. Du Mond's story parallels in a way that pictured by Simmons. Color and composition are both exceedingly grateful to the eye.

The Column of Progress, outside the court, commands the entire north front of the Exposition, as the Tower of Jewels does the southern. (p. 57.) Symmes Richardson, the architect, drew his inspiration from Trajan's Column at Rome, an inspiration so finely bodied forth by the designer and the two sculptors who worked with him, MacNeil and Konti, that this shaft stands as one of the most satisfying creations on the Exposition grounds. Its significance completes the symbolism of the Exposition sculpture and architecture, as the joyous Fountain of Energy at the other end of the north-and-south axis begins it. That fountain celebrates the completion of the Canal. The Tower of Jewels with its sculpture tells the historical story of the conquest of the western seas and their shores. The Court of the Universe is the meeting place of the Nations, come to commemorate the joining of East and West. From this Court, a splendid avenue leads down to the border of the Western Ocean, where stands the Column of Progress, beyond the Exposition. Both in its position and in its sculpture the column signifies that, this celebration over, human endeavor stands ready to go on to still vaster enterprises on behalf of mankind.

The figure atop this Column is the Adventurous Bowman, past human achievement behind him, seeking a new emprise in the West, whither he has loosed his arrow. At his back is a figure of Humanity, signifying the support of mankind. By his side is the woman, ready to crown his success. (p. 58.) The question has often been asked, why there is no string to the archer's bow. The sculptor properly omitted it, for, at the moment the arrow leaves the bow, the cord is vibrating far too strongly to be visible.

The cylindrical frieze below the Bowman represents

the Burden Bearers. This, with the Bowman, is the work of H. A. MacNeil. The spiral of ships ascending the shaft symbolizes the upward course of man's progress. Around the base is the frieze by Isidor Konti, on three sides striving human figures, on the fourth celestial trumpeters announcing victory. The whole signifies man's progress through effort. (p. 60.)

Yet the visitor must not look for a story in all the sculpture here or elsewhere. Some of this art is merely decorative, fulfilling purposes of harmony or completeness in the general mass. The winged figures by Leo Lentelli on the columns before the Arches of the Nations are simply ornaments, relieving, with their shafts, what would otherwise be too sheer a wall in the structure. They may be angels or they may be genii. Decorative, also, are the sculptured medallions between these columns, and the Pegasi on the spandrels of the arch, the medallions done by Calder, the Pegasi by Roth.

The caryatids in pairs of male and female surmounting the balustrade of the sunken garden are merely lamp bearers. The spouting monsters in the fountain pools are but ornamental, and so are the figures in relief under the basins. Those at the base of the shafts are described in detail in the chapter on Fountains. In the decoration of the entablature of the colonnade, the skull of the ox repeated between the garlands recalls the vicissitudes of the pioneers in their long march across the continent.

The Court of the Universe, this huge Piazza of the Nations, is thus all-inclusive. Within its vast oval is room for every theme. From it lead the ways to all the Exposition. In spirit it is as cosmopolitan as the Forum

Ben Macomber

under the Caesars. Its art revives for us

"The glory that was Greece,
The grandeur that was Rome."

Inscriptions in Court of the Universe

I. Arch of the Rising Sun, east side of the Court.

(a) Panel at center of attic, west side of the Arch,
    facing the Court:

The Moon Sinks Yonder in the West While in the East
the Glorius Sun Behind the Dawn Appears. Thus Rise
and Set In Constant Change Those Shining Orbs and
Regulate the Very Life of this Our World.

- Kalidasa, India.

(b) Small panel at right of center, facing the Court:

Our Eyes and Hearts Uplifted Seem to Gaze on
Heavens' Radiance.

- Hitomaro, Japan.

(c) Small panel at left of center, facing the Court:

They Who Know the Truth are Not Equal to Those
Who Love It.

- Confucius, China.

(d) Panel at center of attic, east side of the Arch:

The Balmy Air Diffuses Health and Fragrance. So Tempered is the Genial Glow That We Know Neither Heat Nor Cold. Tulips and Hyacinths Abound. Fostered by A Delicious Clime the Earth Blooms Like A Garden.

- Firdausi, Persia.

(e) Small panel at right of center:

A Wise Man Teaches Be Not Angry. From Untrodden Ways Turn Aside.

- Phra Ruang, Siam.

(f) Small panel at left of center:

He That Honors Not Himself Lacks Honor Wheresoe'er He Goes.

- Zuhayr, Arabia.

II. Arch of the Setting Sun, west side of the Court.

(a) Panel at center of attic, east side of the Arch,
     facing the Court:

Facing West From California's Shores - Inquiring Tireless Seeking What is Yet Unfound - I A Child Very Old Over Waves Toward the House of Maternity the Land of Migrations Look Afar - Look Off the Shores of My Western Sea the Circle Almost Circled.

- Whitman, America.

(b) Small panel at right of center:

Ben Macomber

Truth - Witness of the Past Councilor of the Present Guide of the Future.

- Cervantes, Spain.

(c) Small panel at left of center:

In Nature's Infinite Book of Secrecy A Little I Can Read.

- Shakespeare, England.

(d) Panel at center of attic, west side of the Arch:

It is Absolutely Indispensable For the United States to Effect A Passage From the Mexican Gulf to the Pacific Ocean And I Am Certain That They Will Do It - Would That I Might Live to See it But I Shall Not.

- Goethe, Germany.

(e) Small panel at right of center:

The Universe - An Infinite Sphere the Center Everywhere the Circumference Nowhere.

- Pascal, France.

(f) Small panel at left of center:

The World is in its Most Excellent State When Justice is Supreme.

- Dante, Italy.

VII.

The Court of the Ages
(Officially called "The Court of Abundance.")

An artist's dream in romantic Orientalism - Mullgardt's own title for it - His great "Tower of the Ages" - Mullgardt interprets his architectural masterpiece - Brangwyn's splendid murals, "Earth," "Air," "Fire" and "Water" - The "Fountain of Earth," by Robert Aitken, realism set amidst the romantic.

The Court of the Universe is not Oriental, the Court of the Ages is. Not in architecture, but in feeling, in the atmosphere with which the architect has invested it, this court brings to mind those brilliant lands of the Mediterranean touched by the East through the Moors. You pass under its arcades and walk out into a region of the Sun, warm, bright, dazzling. The architect, Louis Christian Mullgardt, has caught the feeling of the South, - not the rank, jungle South of the tropics; nor the mild, rich South of our own Gulf states; but the hard, brilliant, arid South of the desert. This court expresses Arizona, New Mexico, Spain, Algiers, - lands of the Sun. The very flowers of its first gardens were desert blooms, brilliant in hue, on leafless stalks. There are orange trees, but they, also, are trees of the Sun, smooth of leaf, to retain moisture.

Ben Macomber

It is a court, too, of romance. It might be a garden of Allah, with a plaintive Arab flute singing, among the orange trees, of the wars and the hot passions of the desert. It might be a court in Seville or Granada, with guitars tinkling and lace gleaming among the cool arcades. It is a place for dreams.

The architecture has been called Spanish Gothic, but, according to the architect, it "has not been accredited to any established style." We may well be content to call it simply Mullgardt. The court is an artist's dream, rather than a formal study in historic architecture; and it is the more interesting, as it is the more original, for that. Except for the central fountain, which, fine though it is as a sculptured story, is out of harmony with the filigreed arcades around it, all the sculpture in the court is, in feeling, an intimate part of the romantic architecture. This portion of the art of the court is best considered as decoration, finding its justification in the beauty it imparts to the whole. It has genuine meaning, but what that is remains inscrutable so long as the court is called that of Abundance.

Mullgardt called his creation the "Court of the Ages." He was overruled because the officials deemed the name not in accord with the contemporaneous spirit of the Exposition. They called it the "Court of Abundance." In spite of the name, however, it is not the Court of Abundance. Mullgardt's title gives a key to the cipher of the statues. Read by it, the groups on the altar of the Tower become three successive Ages of Civilization. (See p. 70.)

Tower of the Ages. - This is the most admired of all the Exposition towers, and with reason. The originality, strength and beauty of its design set it above anything else of the sort yet seen in America; and the symbolism of its sculptures, which are the work of Chester Beach, is of almost equal interest with the tower itself. At the base, on the gable above the arch, rude of face and form, with beasts low in the scale, are the people of the Stone Age. Above them is a mediaeval group, the Crusader, the Priest, the Peasant Soldier armed with a cross-bow, with similar figures on the side altars. Enthroned over all, with a crown on her brow, is Modern Civilization, expressed as Intelligence. At her feet are two children, one with an open book, symbolizing Learning; the other, a boy with a part of a machine, representing Industry. The supporting figures on the sides are the Man and Woman of the Present, sprung from the earlier types. The delicate finials rising from the summit of the tower express Aspiration.

The two shafts at the head of the court, each surmounted by a huntress with bended bow, symbolize Earth and Air. Originally they were intended as finials to the double cascade which was to have swept down to the court from the Altar of the Ages on the tower. The cascade was not built, much to the benefit of the beauty of the court, but the ornaments were suffered to remain. The giddy females who support each shaft are sufficiently romantic to be in keeping with the decoration of the court.

The three figures repeated around the top of the arcade are of a hunter dragging a deer, a woman with her offspring on her shoulder, and a primitive man feeding a pelican, all so happily expressed that they are an intimate part of the arcade on which they stand. They seem almost to have grown from their supports. These figures alone, unless we add the florid ladies of the

Ben Macomber

ornamental shafts, with the rich filigree of the arcades and the tower, are all that express in any way the idea of Abundance carried in the present name of the court.

Mullgardt conceived this court as a sermon in stone. Its significance as a whole is best explained by the architect himself. He interprets the court as rising in four horizontal strata:

"The court is an historical expression of the successive Ages of the world's growth. The central fountain symbolizes the nebulous world, with its innate human passions. Out of a chaotic condition came Water (the basin), and Land (the fountain), and Light (the Sun, supported by Helios, and the electroliers). The braziers and cauldrons symbolize Fire. The two sentinel columns to the right and left of the tower symbolize Earth and Air. The eight paintings of the four corners of the ambulatory symbolize the elements of Earth, Air, Fire and Water. The central figure in the North Avenue symbolizes 'Modern Time Listening to the Story of the Ages.'

"The decorative motifs employed on the surrounding arcade are sea-plant life and its animal evolution. The piers, arches, reeds and columns bear legendary decorative motifs of the transition of plant to animal life in the forms of tortoise and other shell motifs; - kelp and its analogy to the prehistoric lobster, skate, crab and sea urchin. The water-bubble motif is carried through all vertical members which symbolize the Crustacean Period, which is the second stratum of the court.

"The third stratum, the prehistoric figures, surmounting the piers of the arcade, also the first group over the tower entrance, show earliest forms of human, animal, reptile and bird life, symbolizing the Stone Age Period.

"The fourth stratum, the second group in the altar tower, symbolizes human struggle for emancipation from ignorance and superstition, in which Religion and War are dominating factors. The kneeling figures on the side altar are similarly expressive. The torches above these mediaeval groups symbolize the Dawn of Understanding. The chanticleers on the finials surrounding the court symbolize the Christian Era. The topmost figure of the altar symbolizes Intelligence, 'Peace on Earth, Good Will Towards All,' the symbols of Learning and Industry at her feet. The topmost figure surmounting the side altar symbolizes Thought. The arched opening forming the enclosure of the altar contains alternating masks expressing Intelligence and Ignorance in equal measure, symbolizing the Peoples of the World. A gradual development to the higher forms of plant life is expressed upward in the altar tower, the conventionalized lily petal being the highest form."

This, then, is the lesson, the deepest and most spiritual attempted in any of the Exposition structures, and surely entitling the court to be called, as its creator wished, the Court of the Ages.

Brangwyn's Murals. - The mural paintings by Frank Brangwyn in the four corners of the arcades are rich, glorious in color, freighted with the opulence of the harvest, but they symbolize the four primeval elements - Earth, Air, Fire and Water. Their themes have nothing to do with Abundance. It is unfortunate that these pictures, far and away the best in the decoration of the Exposition, have been hidden in the corners of a court. The canvases are bold, free, vast as the elements they picture. They need space. When they were unpacked and hung on the walls of Machinery Hall, they were far more effective. Here they are cramped by their close quarters, and easily overlooked. People are not going in to see them as they should, and so are missing one of the chief joys of the Exposition, - the masterpieces of one of the world's greatest living painters.

These representations of the four elements glow and burn with the vivid hues of nature. All of the pictures have a setting of autumn,, that season of the year when nature puts on her dying hues, and floods the earth with color. Their rich reds, purples, yellows, browns, greens and indigoes are the hues of autumn skies, the falling leaves of hardwoods, the dense foliage of pines, colors of the harvest, of fruit and grapes, of flowers, and of deep waters. The men and women in them are primeval, too, of Mediterranean type, and garbed in the barbaric colors in which Southern folk express the warmth of their natures.

Free and vivid as is their color, the breadth of primeval liberty is not less seen in the splendid spaces of Brangwyn's pictures. The forest vistas are illimitable; the air has the freedom of the Golden Age; the skies stretch out and up to heaven.

Each set of two pictures represents one of the elements. The first of the Earth pictures in the northwest corner of the corridor is a harvest of orchard fruits, products of earth. Tall cypresses on the right enhance the vast space of sky over the orchard, the best sky in all the eight paintings. The colors are those of the rich fruits, the autumn flowers, and the garish costumes of Brangwyn's peasantry. The companion picture represents a vintage, with great purple grapes hanging among the bronzing leaves on a trellis, and yellow pumpkins and flowers underfoot. The color is in these, and in the same Southern costumes seen in the first picture.

The first of the Air pictures is as easy to read as the second is difficult. (p. 74.) In it a huge windmill stands on a height against rain-laden clouds and a glowing rainbow. The slope is covered with heavy-headed grain, and stained with vivid flowers, all bending before the swift currents of air. Laborers, men and women, hurry homeward before the wind, from their task of winnowing grain. Boys flying their kites complete the symbolism.

In the companion picture a group of archers are loosing their arrows between the boles of tall, straight hardwoods on the brink of a deep valley. Great white birds are winging outward through the tops of the trees. The distance in the sky beyond is wonderful. The color is of the gorgeous autumn leaves of hardwoods and of rich flowers.

In one of the Water pictures fishermen are drawing a net from a lake suggested by a fringe of purple, white and yellow iris. The men seem to stand on an island or a peninsula, for behind them, beyond tall trees, is a deep indigo lake. Great pregnant clouds float in the sky, and the picture glows with autumn colors.

In the other, men and women come forward with water jars to a source suggested by tall white water birds and flowers growing thick among the sedges. There are the same clouds, big with the promise of rain, and the

Ben Macomber

same profusion of vivid hues.

Primitive Fire is suggested in the next pair by a thick-clustered group of peasants with hands outstretched where a thin column of smoke rises straight. Autumn skies and foliage tell of chill in the air. The colors burn in dying leaves, in the sky, in fruit and grapes. A man is bringing a burden of fagots. Men of bovine anatomy crouch before the fire, their backs arched, their cheeks bulging, as they blow it into flame. These folk are all primitive, candid in their animalism, Samsons in limb and muscle. Brangwyn's mastery of anatomy is notable, and he builds his men with every flexor showing, like a machine.

Pottery burners working around a furnace dimly suggested convey the idea of Industrial Fire in the last of the pictures. There is the same motif of cold in the sky and the fruits, intensified by the somber leafage of fir and pine.

In striking contrast with the light and ethereal quality of the allegorical murals in the arches of the Court of the Universe, these paintings are rich to the point of opulence. There is an enormous depth in them. The figures are full-rounded. The fruits, flowers and grain hang heavily on their steams. The trees bear them-selves solidly. The colors, laid on with strong and heavy strokes, fairly flame in the picture.

Public auction is the fate said to be destined by the Exposition company for these wonderful pictures. It is not to be blamed for this. It is a business corporation, and these paintings are assets on which it may be necessary to realize. But if the company finds itself financially able, it should see to it that the paintings remain in San Francisco as the property of the city. Like the great organ in Festival Hall, which the Exposition has promised to install in the Civic Auditorium when the fair ends, these splendid pictures should be hung in the Auditorium as a gift to the city.

If the Exposition is not able to give them, an opportunity is presented for men of wealth to do art a great service in San Francisco. Our cities, unlike those of Europe and of South America, are not accustomed to buy works of art. Private generosity, then, must supply the deficiency.

In the northern extension of the court, beyond the tower, where the Spanish decoration is carried almost to the bayward facade of the palace group stands a massive female figure, Modern Time Listening to the Story of the Ages. Beyond it are four standards of the Sun, like two at the southern end of the pool in the main court, brilliant at night.

There remains but the central fountain, in the main court, symbolizing the Earth, done by Robert Aitken. (p. 73.) Taken by itself, this is a notable work, but it is not in keeping with the romantic spirit of the Court of Ages. Its figures are magnificently virile, but wholly realistic. Only at night, when, through clouds of rising steam, the globe of the Earth glows red like a world in the making, and from the forked tongues of the climbing serpents flames pour out on the altars set around the pool, - only then does the fountain become mystic. Even then it suggests cosmogony, mechanics, physics, which are not romantic, except in so far as there may be romance of the intellect. However, this is Aitken, not Mullgardt. The allegories of the group are detailed in the chapter on Fountains.

Ben Macomber

VIII.

The Court of the Seasons

A charming bit of Italian Renaissance - Its quiet simplicity - The alcove Fountains of the Seasons, by Furio Piccirilli - Milton Bancroft's Murals - The forecourt, with Evelyn Longman's Fountain of Ceres - Inscriptions.

In The Court of the Seasons, the architect, Henry Bacon of New York, has shown us a charming mood of the Italian Renaissance. (p. 79, 80.) This court, neither too splendid to be comfortable nor too ornate to be restful, is full of a quiet intimacy. Nature's calm is here. It is a little court, and friendly. Its walls are near and sheltering. People like to sit here in the shelter of the close thickets around the still pool in the center. I notice, too, that persons hastening across the grounds come this way, and that they unconsciously slacken pace as they walk through the court.

This is the only one of the three central courts in which everything is in harmony. There is nothing obtrusive about it. The effect is that of a perfect whole, simple, complete. The round pool, smooth, level with the ground, unadorned, gives its note. The colors are warm, the massive pillars softly smooth. The trees press close to the walls, the shrubbery is dense. Birds make happy sounds among the branches. Water falls from the fountains in the alcoves, not with a roar, but with something more than a woodland murmur. These fountains touch one of the purest notes in nature. In cool, high, bare-walled alcoves the water falls in sheets from terrace to terrace, at last into a dark pool below. The sound is steady, gently reinforced by echo from the clean walls behind, and pervasive. It is a very perfect imitation of the sound of mountain waters.

Nothing in this court takes effort. The pictures and the sculpture of the alcoves and the half-dome tell their own story. Here is no elusive mysticism, no obscure symbolism to be dug out with the help of guidebooks, like a hard lesson. The treasures of the Seasons are on the surface, glowing in the face of all.

The Seasons are sheltered in the four alcoves, distinguished from each other only by the fountain groups of Furio Piccirilli and the murals by H. Milton Bancroft. Neither pictures nor statues need much explanation. The first alcove to the left of the half-dome is that of Spring. In the sculptured group of the fountain, flowers bloom and love awakens. It is a fresh and graceful composition. The murals are on the faces of the corridor arches. No one can mistake their meaning. Springtime shows her first blossoms, and the happy shepherd pipes a seasonal air to his flock, now battening on new grass. In the companion picture, Seedtime, are symbols of the spring planting.

Next comes Summer, the time of Fruition. (p. 94.) Above the fountain the mother gives the new-born child to its happy father, and the servant brings the first fruits of the harvest. This is less likable than the other groups. The posture of the mother is not a happy one.

Ben Macomber

The two murals picture Summer and Fruition. Bancroft has taken athletic games as the symbol of the season. Summer is crowning the victor in aquatic sports. Conventional symbols of fruits and flowers represent Fruition.

In the group of Autumn, Providence is the central figure, directing the Harvest. She is bringing in the juice of the grape. The season is significantly represented in the full modeling of the figures and the maturity of the adults. The mural of Autumn, in the rich colors of the dying year, suggests by its symbols of wine and music, the harvest festival. Opposite, is pictured the Harvest, with the garnered crops.

Last of all is Winter, with the bare desolation of the wintry world in the melancholy fountain group. Then Nature rests in the season of conception, while a man sows, his companion having prepared the ground. In his mural of Winter, Bancroft pictures the snowy days, the fuel piled against the cold, the chase of the deer, the spinning in the long evenings. The companion piece represents the festival side of the season, when men have time to play. The Seasons are complete.

On the walls of the half-dome are two formal paintings by Bancroft, conventional but charming in their allegory. These are Bancroft's best murals. In the first, Time crowns Art, while her handmaids, Painting, Pottery, Weaving, Glass-making, Metal-working and Jewel-making, stand in attendance. In the other, Man is taught the laws of Love, Life, and Death, Earth, Fire, and Water.

On the summit of the half-dome is a group representing the Harvest, and before it, on two splendid columns, are Rain, a woman bearing the cup of the waters, and Sunshine, another with a palm branch. All three are by Albert Jaegers. At the other extremity of the court each of the two pylons is surmounted by a bull, wreathed in garlands, and led by man and maiden to the sacrifice. These groups, each called the Feast of the Sacrifice, are also by Albert Jaegers. (p. 79.) The spandrels on the arches and the female figures on the cornices are by his brother, August Jaegers.

The abundance of the Seasons is symbolized in the fruit-bearing figures that form the pilasters of the cornices of the arches, and by the fat ears of corn depending from the Ionic capitals of the columns. These types of fruitfulness have a further justification in the neighborhood of the Palaces of Agriculture and Food Products, which border the court on the north.

The eastern and western arches are exquisite in their simple proportion, and the delicate charm of the fresco of their vaulted passages. The quality of this interior decoration is enhanced by the beauty of the staff work, which throughout this court is the most successful found in the Exposition. Here this plaster is soft, rich and warm, and looks more real and permanent than elsewhere.

I prefer to consider the northern approach between the two palaces as not a part of this court. The pleasant intimacy of the court would have been enhanced if it had been cut off from this approach by an arch. Half way down the forecourt is the formal fountain of Ceres by Evelyn Beatrice Longman, which must cheer the hearts of those who would have all art draped.

Inscriptions in Court of Seasons

(a) On arch at east side:

So Forth Issew'd the Seasons of
The Yeare - First Lusty Spring All
Dight in Leaves and Flowres.
Then Came the Jolly Sommer Being Dight
In A Thin Silken Cassock Coloured Greene.
Then Came the Autumne All in Yellow Clad.
Lastly Came Winter Cloathed All in Frize
Chattering His Teeth For Cold that Did Him Chill.

- Spenser.

(b) On arch at west side:

For Lasting Happiness We Turn
Our Eyes To One Alone
And She Surrounds You Now.
Great Nature Refuge of the
Weary Heart And Only Balm To
Breasts That Have Been Bruised.
She Hath Cool Hands For Every
Fevered Brow And Gentlest
Silence For the Troubled Soul.

- Sterling.

IX.

The Courts of Flowers and Palms

The Court of Flowers typically Italian - Its delightful garden and fountain, "Beauty and the Beast," by Edgar Walter - Borglum's fine group, "The Pioneer" - The Court of Palms is Grecian in feeling - "The End of the Trail," by Fraser, a chapter in American history - Murals in the doorways - Arthur Mathews' "Triumph of Culture."

Recessed in the south front of the palace group, and leading back to the Court of the Seasons and the Court of the Ages, are two perfect smaller courts, each admirably living up to its name - the Court of Flowers and the Court of Palms. (See p. 85, 88, 93.) Both courts were designed by George W. Kelham. Each is a pleasant and colorful bay of sunshine facing southward between two graceful towers. One is bright with level fields of flowers, the other cool with greensward and palms set about a sunken garden. Both are calm, peaceful spots to rest and dream in the sun. Both are of the South. Here summer first unfolds her robes, and here she longest tarries.

Though at first sight these courts are much alike, they differ in feeling and effect. The Court of Flowers is Italian, the Court of Palms Grecian, though Grecian

Ben Macomber

with an exuberance scarcely Athenian. Perhaps there is something Sicilian in the warmth of its decoration. When it is bright and warm, the Court of Palms is most Greek in feeling; less so on duller days.

But the Court of Flowers is Italian in all moods. With its shady balcony above the colonnade, it might be in Verona or Mantua. It is a graceful court, formal, yet curiously informal. Its paired Corinthian columns, its conventional lions by the porches and its flower girls around the balcony, its lamp standards and the sculptured fountain, go with formal gardens. The garden here is itself formal in its planting, and yet so simple, so natural, that it banishes all ceremony.

This garden is one of the best things in the truly wonderful floral show at the Exposition. The flowers are massed as we always dream of seeing them in the fields, - a dream never quite so well realized before. The areas of the court in the Exposition's opening weeks were solid fields of daffodils, thick as growing wheat, with here and there a blood-red poppy, set to accent the yellow gold of the mass. Other flowers have now replaced these in an equal blaze of color. Here, too, are free, wild clumps of trees and shrubs, close set, with straggling outposts among the flowers, as natural as those bordering grain fields in California valleys.

It is a summery court, lacking but one thing to make it ideally perfect. It ought to have crickets and cicadas in it, to rasp away as the warm afternoons turn into evening, and tree hylas to make throaty music in the still, rich-lighted night.

The statuary goes well with the court. There is a pretty, summery grace about the flower girls designed by

Calder for the niches above the colonnade, and in the figures of Edgar Walter's central fountain. Here on the fountain are Beauty and the Beast, Beauty clad in a summer hat and nothing else, the Beast clothed in ugliness. (p. 100.) Never mind the story. This is Beauty, and Beauty needs no story. Four airy pipers, suggestive at least of the song of the cicada on long, hot afternoons, support the fountain figure. Around the basin of the pool is carved in low relief a cylindrical frieze of tiger, lion and bear, and, wonder of wonders, Hanuman, the Monkey King of Hindoo mythology, leading the bear with one hand and prodding the lion with the other.

Before the court The Pioneer sits his horse, a thin, sinewy, nervous figure; old, too, - as old as that frontier which has at last moved round the world. (See p. 87.) The statue, which is by Solon Borglum, is immensely expressive of that hard, efficient type of frontiersmen who, scarcely civilized, yet found civilization always dogging their footsteps as they moved through the wilderness and crossed the deserts. He is, indeed, the forerunner of civilization, sent forward to break ground for new states. This group is offset against that other fine historical sculpture, The End of the Trail, placed before the Court of Palms. As representatives of the conquering and the conquered race, the two must be studied together.

The elusive Grecian feeling of the Court of Palms comes in large part from the simple Ionic columns, and the lines of the gabled arches. Properly, this court is in the Italian Renaissance, but it is less Italian than the Court of Flowers. Like that court, it is warm and sunny, full of color and gladness. It has the same harmonious perfection, but it is more formal. Its

Ben Macomber

sunken garden is bordered with a conventional balustrade and grass slopes, with marble seats by the paths. There is no fountain, only a long pool in the sunken area, and a separate raised basin at the inner end with gently splashing jets, giving out a cool and peaceful sound. Fat decorated urns, instead of lions, guard the entrances to the buildings. Italian cypresses border the court, with formal clipped acacias in boxes between the pillars of the colonnade.

The Fountain of Beauty and the Beast, which stands in the Court of Flowers, was designed to be set here, while Mrs. Harry Payne Whitney's Fountain of the Arabian Nights was to have found a place in the Court of Flowers. These two courts were planned as the homes of the fairy tales, one of Oriental, the other of Occidental lore. Many beautiful things were designed for them. The attic of the Court of Flowers, which was intended as the place of Oriental Fairy Tales, was to have carried sculptured stories from the Arabian Nights. But none of these things was done. Mrs. Whitney's fountain was modeled but never made, unfortunately, for the modeled figures are charming.

The only sculpture in the Court of Palms, aside from the "End of the Trail," which stands before it, is in the decoration of the entablature and the arches. Horned and winged female caryatids mark off the entablature into garlanded panels. All the three arches under the gables are enriched with figures of women and of children supporting a shield, conventional groups, but graceful.

"The End of the Trail," by James Earle Fraser, of New York, is a great chapter in American history, told in noble sculpture. The dying Indian, astride his exhausted cayuse, expresses the hopelessness of the Red Man's battle against civilization. (p. 86.) There is more significance and less convention, perhaps, in this than in any other piece of Exposition sculpture. It has the universal touch. It makes an irresistible appeal.

To make up for the lack of statuary in this court there are mural paintings over the entrances leading into the Palaces of Education and Liberal Arts on either hand, and into the Court of the Seasons. Of these three lunettes two add little to the beauty of the court except for the vivid touch of color which they give it. One, over the door of the Palace of Education, is entitled "Fruits and Flowers," by Childe Hassam. It is a triumph of straight line applied to the female form. Over the door of the Palace of Liberal Arts is "The Pursuit of Pleasure," ascribed to Charles Holloway. The figures are gracefully drawn, the coloring flowery. There is better quality in Arthur F. Mathews' "Triumph of Culture," over the entrance to the Court of Seasons. In color and force this comes nearer to the splendid standard set by Frank Brangwyn than anything else in the Exposition's mural decoration. Perhaps that is too faint praise, for this is a real picture. In it a victorious golden spirit, crowding aside brute force, allows the Humanities, representatives of Culture, to triumph as the guardians of Youth. The figures are human, there is strength and ease in them, and the color is a deep-toned song.

Ben Macomber

X.

The Fountains

A characteristic and fitting feature of the Exposition - Fountain of Energy - The Mermaids - Gertrude Vanderbilt Whitney's "El Dorado" and Mrs. Burroughs' "Youth" - Rising and Setting Sun - Piccirilli's "Seasons" - Aitken's masterpiece, the Fountain of Earth - "Beauty and the Beast."

The fountain, the spring, the well, is a characteristic note in the life and art of all lands in the Sun. The Arabians, the Moors, the Spaniards, the Italians and the Greeks loved fountains. It is less so in the North, in the regions of much rain, where water flows naturally everywhere. But nothing is so welcome in a thirsty land as a fountain. Hence there is appropriateness in the many fountains of this Exposition, which reflects in its plan the walled cities of the Orient of the Mediterranean, where fountains play in the courts of palaces, in public squares and niches in the walls; and pools lie by the mosques, and in the gardens.

Here are many kinds of fountains, from huge masses of sculpture spouting forth many powerful streams in the sun to terraced basins where water murmurs in quiet alcoves, and simple jets tinkling in summery courts. Of those fountains that have especially been dignified and adorned by sculpture there are fourteen, some single, some in pairs, with one quartet in the Court of Seasons. Their sequence from the chief gate of the Exposition follows in a way the symbolic significance of all the sculpture.

The Fountain of Energy, by A. Stirling Calder, in the center of the South Gardens before the Tower of Jewels, as a figure of aquatic triumph, celebrates the completion of the Panama Canal. (See p. 47.) Resting on a pedestal in the center of the pool, and supported by a circle of figures representing the dance of the oceans, is the Earth, surmounted by a figure of Energy, the force that dug the canal. Fame and Victory blow their bugles from his shoulders. When all the jets are playing, Energy, horsed, rides through the waters on either hand.

The band around the Earth, decorated with sea horses and fanciful aquatic figures, represents the seaway now completed around the globe. On one side a bull-man, a rather weak-chinned minotaur, stands for the strength of Western civilization; on the other, a cat-woman represents the civilization of the Eastern hemisphere. Surrounding the central figure in the pool are the four Oceans, - the Atlantic with corraled tresses and sea horses in her hand, riding a helmeted fish; the Northern Ocean as a Triton mounted on a rearing walrus; the Southern Ocean as a negro backing a sea elephant and playing with an octopus; and the Pacific as a female on a creature that might be a sea lion, but is not. Dolphins backed by nymphs of the sea serve a double purpose as decoration and as spouts for the waters.

The central figure of this fountain has been severely criticized, and with reason. The design is a beautiful

Ben Macomber

one, but unfortunately not well adapted to reproduction on so large a scale. Symbolism is here carried to an extreme that spoils the simplicity which alone makes a really great work imposing. Calder had a fine idea of a figure of joyous triumph to stand as the opening symbol of the festival side of the Exposition. He deserves credit for the real beauty of his design. It is a pity that a thing so charming as a model should not have worked out well in heroic proportions.

As a fountain, though, it is splendid. The pool and its spouting figures are glorious. The play of the waters when all the jets are spouting is not only magnificent but unique. This veil of water shooting out and falling in a half sphere about the globe has not been seen before. There is a real expression of energy in the force of the leaping streams.

Mermaid Fountains, by Arthur Putnam. - At the far end of each of the lovely pools in the South Gardens is an ornamental fountain of ample basins topped by a graceful mermaid, behind whose back a fish spouts up a single jet of water. These are formal fountains, but exceedingly harmonious. Without trying to be pretentious, they achieve an effect of
simple beauty. (p. 99.)

"El Dorado" and "Youth." - Within the colonnaded wings of the Tower of Jewels are two fountains which carry' out the symbolism of the days of the Spanish explorers in their themes, the Aztec myth of El Dorado, and the fabled Fountain of Youth, sought by Ponce de Leon. In their way, these are the loveliest fountains on the Exposition grounds, though they differ so from all the rest that comparison is not easy. The naïve conception of the Fountain of Youth and the realistic strength of that of El Dorado lead visitors back to them again and again. They are hidden fountains, as their prototypes were hidden. Each terminates one of the two open colonnades with a central niche composition flanked on either hand by a sculptured frieze. Each is the work of a woman sculptor, and both, though very different, are far from the conventional or the commonplace.

The Fountain of El Dorado, by Gertrude Vanderbilt Whitney, tells the story of an Aztec myth of a god whose brilliance is so dazzling that the sun is his veil, and who lives in a darkened temple lest his light destroy humanity. (p. 54.) At the center of the recessed wall are doors of the deity's shaded abode, a guardian on either side. In the friezes naked humanity moves ever onward, striving to reach the home of the god. The figures, in full relief, are splendid in their grace and vigor. Here are men and women whom nothing can hold back; here are those who must be pushed along, some who linger for love, others for worldly goods; but all, the strong and the faint, the eager and the tardy, move forward irresistibly to their destiny.

In Wait's "The Stories of El Dorado," the following account is given of this aboriginal myth of an expected Indian Messiah, El Hombre Dorado, the Gilded Man, as the Spaniards interpreted the native words, - which played a fateful part in the history of the primitive races of Spanish America:

"No words incorporated into the English language have been fraught with such stupendous consequences as El Dorado. When the padres attempted to tell the story of the Christ, the natives exclaimed 'El Dorado' - the golden. The ignorant sailors and adventurers seized upon the literal meaning, instead of the spiritual one. The time, being that of Don Quixote and of the Inquisition, accounts for the childish credulity on one side and the unparalleled ferocity on the other. The search for El Dorado, whether it was believed to be a fabulous country of gold, or an inaccessible mountain, or a lake, or a city, or a priest who anointed himself with a fragrant oil and sprinkled his body with fine gold dust, must always remain one of the blackest pages in the history of the white race. The great heart of humanity will ever ache with sympathy for the melancholy and pitiful end of the natives, who at the time of the conquest of Mexico were confidently expecting the return of the mild and gentle Quetzalcoatl, - the Mexican variant of this universal myth. * * * The Golden Hearted came from an island in the East, and to this he returned, in the legend. In all variants, he gave a distinct promise of return. This accounts for the awe inspired by Europeans in the minds of the natives, causing them everywhere to fall easy victims of the unscrupulous adventurers swarming into their country. Fate never played a more cruel prank than to have one race of men speak and act constantly from the standpoint of tradition, while the other thought solely of material gain."

Interesting, too, is Mrs. Edith Woodman Burroughs' conception of the Fountain of Youth. (p. 53.) The beautiful central figure is a girl child standing without self-consciousness by blooming primroses. Modeled faintly on the pedestal are the parents, from whose upturned faces and uplifted hands the primroses seem to spring. In the friezes, wistful old people are borne onward to Destiny in boats manned by joyous chubby children, unconscious of their priceless gift of youth to which their elders look back with so much longing.

Fountains in the Court of the Universe. - Passing through the Tower of Jewels into the great court where themes become universal under the circle of stars above the surrounding colonnade, we come to the Fountains of the Rising and the Setting Sun, by A. A. Weinmann, one at either focus of the elliptical sunken garden. In the East, the Sun, in the strength of the morning, his wings spread for flight, is springing upward from the top of the tall column rising out of the fountain. Walk toward him from the west and you get the effect of his rising. (p. 69.)

At his feet a garland of children is woven in the form of a ring at the top of the column. At the base of the shaft, just above the basin, is a cylindrical frieze in low relief, symbolizing Day Triumphant. Weinmann interprets this as the Spirit of Time, hour-glass in hand, followed by the Spirit of Light with flaming torch, while Energy trumpets the approaching day. Interwoven with these figures is an allegory of Truth with mirror and sword, escaping from the sinister power of Darkness, Falsehood shrinking from its image in the mirror of Truth, and Vice struggling in the coils of a serpent. It is not easy to read either series, or to disentangle one from the other.

In the West the Setting Sun is just alighting, with folding wings. The luminary, which in the morning was male, to represent the essentially masculine spirit, the upwardness and onwardness of opening day, has now become female in its quality of brooding evening. In fact, this same figure, which the sculptor shows in the Palace of Fine Arts, is there called by him "Descending Night."

The frieze at the base of the shaft of the Setting Sun is

as difficult to interpret as the other. On it are shown the Gentle Powers of Night. Dusk folds in her cloak Love, Labor and Peace. Next are Illusions borne on the wings of Sleep, then the Evening Mists, followed by the Star Dance, and lastly, Luna, the goddess of the Silver Crescent. Luna may be recognized, for the Silver Crescent is in her hand; and, with the sequence I have just given, you may recognize the others.

The figures supporting the basins and the creatures in the pools of each fountain are merely decorative. The play of water in these fountains is joyous and delightful. The purpose of a fountain is well and adequately fulfilled.

There now remain the seven fountains of the lesser courts, connected more or less intimately in theme with their immediate surroundings.

In the Court of Seasons. - Four are in the Court of Seasons, where Spring, Summer, Autumn and Winter, by Furio Piccirilli, have each its own alcove in the wall and its own play of water. These are pleasant fountains, simple and quiet. There is some feeling of lonely mountain cliffs in the plain walls behind them, hung with streamers of the maidenhair vine.

In the first alcove stands Spring with her flowers; on one side the man, in whom love awakens, on the other fresh young Flora, bringing the first offerings of the year. Next comes the alcove of Summer, the time of fruition. The mother brings her babe to its father, the laborer bears the first fruits of the harvest. (p. 94.)

Autumn follows, the time of harvest. The central figure of the fountain group is Providence. The fruits of the year are brought in, and the vintage is in progress. Last of all comes Winter, the melancholy time when the trees are bare and the bark splits with the frost. The central figure is naked Nature resting in the period of conception. On one side is bowed an old man, after preparing the ground for the seed; on the other is a strong man sowing. This is perhaps the best of the four fountain groups it expresses admirably the bleakness and sadness of the season. There is a wintry chill about it, the gloom of a dark December day. Of the others, Spring is most likable, with its conception of the seasonal impulse to love; and Autumn, for the strength of its figures and the beauty of their modeling.

In the forecourt, appropriately placed between the Palaces of Agriculture and Food Products, stands the Fountain of Ceres. (p. 79.) It is an odd fountain, with the water gushing from the mouths of satyrs set barely above the level of the ground, as though for the watering of small animals. Ceres stands above, with a wreath of cereals and a scepter of corn. The frieze pictures the dance of joyous nature.

Fountain of Earth. - In Mullgardt's Court of Ages is the Fountain of Earth, by Robert Aitken, the most magnificently virile of all the Exposition fountains, conceived of a powerful imagination and executed in strength and beauty. (p. 70, 73.)

The sculpture of the fountain must be described in three parts. Aitken's own interpretation is condensed in the following account. On the wall of the parapet at the foot of the pool, sixty feet from the central structure, is a colossal figure symbolizing Helios, in his arms the great globe of the setting sun after it has thrown off the nebulous mass that subsequently became the earth. The

Ben Macomber

whole expresses primitive man's idea of the splashing of the sun into the water as it sets.

On the side of the central structure toward the figure of Helios, and leading up to the Earth, are two groups, each of five crouching figures, and divided by a conventional plane. At the outer extremity, Destiny, in the shape of two enormous hands and arms, gives life with one and takes it with the other. The five figures on the left side represent the Dawn of Life, those on the right, the Fullness and End of Existence. The first group begins with a woman asleep, just from the hand of Destiny; while the succeeding figures symbolize the Awakening, the Joy of Being, finally, the Kiss of Life, with the human pair offering their children, representing the beginnings of fecundity.

On the east side, a figure of Greed looks back on the earth, the mass in his hands suggesting the futility of worldly possessions. Next is a group of Faith, wherein a patriarch holds forth to the woman the hope of immortality, with a scarab, ancient symbol of renewed life. Then comes a man of Sorrow, as the woman with him falls into her last Slumber. These are about to be drawn into oblivion by the relentless hand of Destiny. The gap between these groups and the main structure of the fountain typifies the unknown time between the beginning of things and the dawn of history.

Each of the four panels in pierced relief surrounding the globe of the Earth tells a single story, with the exception of the first, which tells three. Traveling to the left around the globe, we begin with the figure of Vanity, mirror in hand, in the center of the first panel, as the symbol of worldly motive. Here, too, are primitive man and woman, bearing their burdens, symbolized by their progeny, into the unknown future, ready to meet whatever be the call of earth. The woman suggests the overwhelming instincts of motherhood.

Passing into the next panel, we see their children, now grown, finding themselves, with Natural Selection. The man in the center, splendid in physical and intellectual perfection, attracts the women on either hand, while two other men, deserted for this finer type, display anger and despair. One tries to hold the woman by force, the other, unable to comprehend, turns hopelessly away.

The succeeding panel symbolizes the Survival of the Fittest. Here physical strength begins to play its part, and the war spirit awakens, with woman as its cause. The chiefs struggle for supremacy, while their women try in vain to separate them.

The last panel portrays the Lesson of Life. The elders offer to hotheaded youth the benefit of their experience. The beautiful woman in the center draws to her side the splendid warrior, whose mother on his left gives her affectionate advice. On the right of the panel, a father restrains a wayward and jealous youth who has been rejected by the female.

Passing again into the first panel we find a representation of Lust, - a man struggling to embrace a woman, who shrinks from his caresses. Thus the circle is complete; these last two figures, though in the first panel, are separated from those first described by decorations on the upper and lower borders.

Ben Macomber

Framing the panels, while also indicating the separation in time of their stories, stand archaic figures of Hermes, such as the ancients employed to mark distances on the roads. Their outstretched hands hold up the beginnings of life in the form of rude primeval beasts, from whose mouths issue the jets of the fountain.

At night this fountain glows deep red, from lamps concealed within the panels, while clouds of rosy steam rising around the globe create an illusion of a world in the making.

The Fountain of Beauty and the Beast was originally intended for the Court of Palms, which was conceived as the Court of Occidental Fairy Tales, just as the Court of Flowers was to have been that of Oriental Fairy Tales. Mrs. Whitney's fountain of the Arabian Nights, a creation of whimsical beauty, was to have stood in the latter court. It was modeled, but was never enlarged; and its place was taken by Beauty and the Beast, the work of Edgar Walter. (p. 100.)

This is another harmonious fountain, rightly conceived, so that its sculpture does not overbalance its use in the play of water, and admirably in tune with the flowery grace of the court. Beauty, pouring water from a Greek amphora, sits lightly upon the ugly Beast. Why she wears a smart Paris hat no one has discovered. Four cheery pipers, lively as crickets in the sun, support the upper bowl. Around the lower basin is a frieze in low relief, figuring Hanuman, the King of Monkeys, leading a bear with one hand and prodding a lion with the other. All this is part of the original fairy-tale significance of the court.

The fountains are of the glories of the Exposition. There is always charm in the movement of the waters, rest in their music. The appeal is elemental, and therefore, universal. Artificial jets can never equal the play of water in Nature, but when adorned with harmonious sculpture, as here, they become that significant and satisfying imitation which is Art.

Ben Macomber

XI.

The Palace of Machinery

A vast rectangular hall, saved by Ward's successful architecture from being a huge barn - Modeled on the Roman Baths of Caracalla - Patigian's finely decorative sculptures, symbolizing the mechanical forces and labor - Beauty of the interior - A Cathedral of Dynamics.

A mighty hall is the Palace of Machinery. (See p. 105, 106.) Beachey flew in it. The Olympic might rest in its center aisle with clear space at both bow and stern, and room in the side aisles for two ocean greyhounds as large as the Mauretania. Vastness is the note of the architecture which Clarence Ward has employed to give body to this enormous space. It is an architecture of straight lines in all the outer structure, lending itself admirably to the expression of enormous proportions. In general ground plans the palace is a simple rectangular hall. Think, then, of the task the architect had before him to avoid making the palace a huge barn. His work succeeded, as any great work succeeds, because he used simple means.

First of all, a Roman model was well chosen for so vast a building. The Greeks built no large roofed structures. Their great assemblages were held in open-air theaters and stadia. The Greek masterpiece, the incomparable Parthenon at Athens, was considerably smaller than Oregon's timbered imitation at the Exposition. On the other hand, the solid Roman style lends itself to bulk. The models followed in the Machinery Palace were the Roman Baths, particularly the Baths of Caracalla. They have been used once before as a model in this country, in the building of the Pennsylvania Railway station in New York. There, too, travertine was first successfully imitated by Paul Deniville. Looking at the Palace of Machinery, indeed, it is not difficult to imagine it as the noble metropolitan terminal of a great railway system. It would hold many long passenger trains, and an army of travelers. The distinctive feature of the perspective is the triple gable at the ends of the palace and over the great main entrance. By thus breaking up the long roof lines, as well as by lowering the flanks of the building to flat-roofed wings, a barn like effect was avoided. In the triple gables, also, the three central aisles which distinguish the interior show in the outer structure. Under the gables the huge clerestory windows above the entrances relieve the great expanse of the end walls. Similar windows open up the walls above the flat-topped wings. In the main entrance, the gables are deepened to form a huge triple vestibule where the row of columns is repeated. The long side walls are relieved by pairs of decorated columns flanking the minor entrances.

Thus, by entirely simple devices, the long lines and vast expanses of wall are deprived of monotony. The architect has given majesty to the palace, not merely a majesty of hugeness, but of just proportions and dignified simplicity. In the general architectural scheme of the Exposition it forms one end of the main

Ben Macomber

group of palaces, at the other end of which is set the Palace of Fine Arts. Machinery Hall, with its severe massiveness and solidity, is a balance to the poetry and spirituality of the Fine Arts.

The main entrance is on the west side, looking down the avenue between the Palaces of Mines and Varied Industries. Perhaps it is better, though, to take a first view of the sculptural decoration at the entrance at either the north or the south end, where almost everything is shown that appears in the more complicated main vestibule.

The three clerestory windows make three arches with four piers. In front of each pier stands a great Sienna column crowned with one of four symbolic figures, each, in the strength of the male, emblematic of force. First on the left is "Electricity," grasping the thunderbolt, and standing with one foot on the earth, signifying that electricity is not only in the earth but around it. The man with the lever that starts an engine represents "Steam Power." "Imagination," the power which conceives the thing "Invention" bodies forth, stands with eyes closed; its force comes from within. Wings on his head suggest the speed of thought. At his feet is the Eagle of Inspiration. "Invention" bears in his hand a winged figure, - Thought, about to rise in concrete form.

The eagle appears as a symbol of the United States, on the entablature carried across the opening below the arch on two Corinthian columns in each embrasure. The lower third of each of these shafts is decorated with a cylindrical relief representing the genii of machinery, flanked by human toilers and types of machines. The genii are blind, as the forces developed by machines are blind. There are only two of these cylindrical friezes, but they are repeated many times on the columns at either end and at the main entrance, and on the pairs of columns that flank the minor openings in the western wall.

Over the main entrance the gable is extended to enclose a majestic triple vestibule, backed by the same effect that appears at the palace ends, but with the entablature and its supporting columns repeated across the outer arches. (p. 111.) With the exception of the spandrels on the transverse arches, the sculptural decoration here is the same as that described for the end entrances, though more often repeated. The spandrels represent the application of power to machines. All this decoration is the work of Haig Patigian, of San Francisco.

Before the main entrance stands the only example, in the Exposition sculpture, of the work of the dean of American sculptors, Daniel Chester French. This is his noteworthy group, the Genius of Creation. (p. 147.) Other statues by French will be found among the exhibits of the Fine Arts Palace. The Genius of Creation was placed here at the last moment. It had been intended for the Court of the Universe, while Douglas Tilden's group of "Modern Civilization" was to have stood before the Palace of Machinery. When this was not completed, the Exposition wisely decided that the great court already had enough statuary, and ordered French's group erected in its place.

According to French himself, this group might well have been called "The Angel of Generation." The winged figure, neither male nor female, but angelic, is veiled, suggesting the creative impulse as a blind

Ben Macomber

command from unknown sources. The arms are raised in a gesture of creative command. It has wings, said French, because. both art and the conception demanded these spiritual symbols. The man and woman against the rock whereon the angel sits are emblems of the highest types created. The man looks upward and outward with one hand clenched, ready to grapple with life. The woman reaches out for sympathy and support; her fingers find this in the hand of the man at the back of the rock. Man and woman are encircled by the snake, the earliest symbol of eternity and reproduction, a figure appearing, curiously enough, in every religion, and with much the same significance.

Without ignoring the majesty of the exterior, glowing with color and adorned with statuary, it may be said that the real nobility of this great structure appears in the splendid timber work of the interior. Here, where every bone and rib of the huge hall stands bare as the builders left it, is a note of true grandeur. The long rows of great timbered columns, the lofty arches that spring from them, the almost endless vista of truss and girder, tell of vastness that cannot be expressed by the finished architecture outside. The finest character of the palace is within. From the outside it is a great and well-proportioned hall. Within it becomes a vast cathedral, dedicated to the mighty spirit of Dynamics.

XII.

The Palace of Fine Arts and its Exhibit,
With the Awards

A memorable demonstration of the value of landscape to architecture - Simplicity the foundation of
Maybeck's achievement - The Colonnade and Rotunda
- Altar, Friezes and Murals - Equestrian statue of
Lafayette - Night views - The Palace should be made
permanent in Golden Gate Park - The Fine Arts
Exhibit - Its contemporaneous character and great
general merit - American art well shown - The foreign
collections - Sweden's characteristically national art -
Exhibits of France, Italy, Holland, Argentina, and other
countries - Japan and China exhibit ancient as well as
modern art - The Annex - Work of the Futurists -
Notable sculptures in the Colonnade - Grand Prizes,
Medals of Honor and Gold Medals Awarded.

If everything else in the beautiful architecture of the
Exposition were forgotten, the memory of the Palace
of Fine Arts would remain. It should be a source of
pride to every Californian that this incomparable
building is the work of a Californian, and a source of
deep satisfaction to the architect himself that it so
completely points the lesson which he intended it to
convey. For the Palace of Fine Arts is a sermon in
itself. In it old Roman models have been used to

Ben Macomber

elaborate a California text. Its structure and setting are the demonstration of a theorem, - the finished word of the preachment of a lifetime. The Exposition gave the preacher his opportunity. Bernard Maybeck, the Berkeley architect, had long been telling California that architecture here, to be beautiful, needed only to be an effective background for landscape. His theory is that as trees and plants grow so easily and so quickly here, Californians are wasting their finest source of beauty if they do not combine landscape with building.

When Maybeck was called upon to design a palace of fine arts at the Exposition, one fact enabled him to exemplify his theory in the finest way. The old Harbor View bog was found to have a bottom impervious enough to hold water, and the trees of the demolished resort were still standing. When the mud was scooped out, a lake was left. That gave not only growing trees, in addition to the resources of the Exposition's forestry, but also a real sheet of water, for the landscape. (See p.112.)

Maybeck surprised me by saying that there is nothing specially remarkable about the Palace itself. "What is it the people like?" he asked, and himself replied, "it is the water and the trees." When I reminded him of the beauty of the colonnade seen from points in the enclosed passageway, where no water is in view, he answered: "The public was bribed to like that. Leaving off the roof between the colonnade and the gallery was a direct bribe. A few other simple devices give the effect the people like. One of these is the absence of windows in the walls, a device well known to the old Italians. Others are the water, the trees, and the flower-covered pergolas on the roof."

Maybeck's modesty is genuine, but he deserves more credit than he gives himself. I quote him because his point is worth emphasizing. The highest beauty can be attained by simple means. If all our architects could see that, we should have less straining for effect, less over doneness, and more harmony and significance in our buildings. The people can and do appreciate this kind of beauty. It was surely inspiration that made it possible for Maybeck to produce this masterpiece.

Sweeping in a great arc around the western shore of the lagoon, the Palace, in the architect's view, is merely a background for the water, the trees and the plants on the terraced walls and pergolas. Certainly it is a beautiful setting to a beautiful scene. So perfectly are the Palace and its foreground fitted to each other that the structure looks as though it might have stood there for twenty centuries, a well-preserved Roman villa, while generations of trees grew, and decayed, and were reproduced around its base.

The great detached colonnade, with its central rotunda, is the climax of the entire structure. It is backed up and given solidity by the walls of the gallery behind it, 1,100 feet long. These walls, unbroken save for the entrances, are relieved and beautified by shrubbery set on a terrace halfway between the ground and the eaves. (p. 113.) At the extremities of the double colonnade, and spaced regularly along it, are groups of four columns, each crowned with a great box designed for flowers and vines. Unfortunately, the architect's plan to place growing plants in these receptacles was vetoed because of the cost. The weeping women at the corners, by Ulric Ellerhusen, expressive of the melancholy felt on leaving a great art collection, were intended to be only half seen through drooping vines.

On the water side of the rotunda, a novel effect of inclusion is obtained by semi-circular walls of growing mesembryanthemum.

Around the entablature of the noble octagonal rotunda are repeated Bruno Louis Zimm's three panels, representing "The Struggle for the Beautiful." (p. 114.) In one, Art, as a beautiful woman, stands in the center, while on either side the idealists struggle to hold back the materialists, here conceived as centaurs, who would trample upon Art. In another, Bellerophon is about to mount Pegasus. Orpheus walks ahead with his lyre, followed by a lion, representing the brutish beasts over whom music hath power. Back in the procession come Genius, holding aloft the lamp, and another figure bearing in one hand the pine cones of immortality, in the other a carved statue which she holds forward as a lesson in art to the youth before her. In the third panel appears Apollo, god of all the arts, in the midst of a procession of his devotees bearing garlands. Between the panels are repeated alternately male and female figures, symbolizing those who battle for the arts.

On an altar before the rotunda, overlooking the lagoon, kneels Robert Stackpole's figure of Venus, representing the Beautiful, to whom all art is servant. The panel in front of the altar is by Bruno Louis Zimm, and pictures Genius, the source of Inspiration. Unfortunately, this fine altar has been made inaccessible; it can be seen only from across the lagoon. (p. 137.) The friezes decorating the huge circular flower receptacles set around the base of the rotunda and at intervals in the colonnade are by Ellerhusen. Eight times repeated on the lofty columns within the rotunda is "The Priestess of Culture," a conventional but pleasing sculpture by Herbert Adams.

Above, in the dome, Robert Reid's eight murals, splendid in color, are too far away to be seen well as pictures. Two separate series are alternated, one symbolizing the Progress of Art, the other depicting the Four Golds of California. The panel in the east, nearest the altar, is "The Birth of European Art." The sacred fire burns on an altar, beside which stands the guardian holding out the torch of inspiration to an earthly messenger who leans from his chariot to receive it. On the right is the Orange panel, representing one of the California golds.

"Inspiration in All Art" comes next. The veil of darkness, drawn back, reveals the arts: Music, Painting, Poetry, and Sculpture. A winged figure bears the torch of inspiration. The second of the California golds, the Wheat panel, follows, and then "The Birth of Oriental Art." The allegory here is the ancient Ming legend of the forces of earth trying to wrest inspiration from the powers of air. A Chinese warrior mounted on a dragon struggles with an eagle.

Gold, the yellow metal, is the subject of the next panel, followed by "Ideals in Art." In this appear concrete symbols of the chief motives of art, the classic nude of the Greeks, the Madonna and Child of Religion, Joan of Arc for Heroism, Youth and Material Beauty represented by a young woman, and Absolute Nature by the peacock. A mystic figure in the background holds the cruse wherewith to feed the sacred flame. A winged figure bears laurels for the living, while the shadowy one in the center holds the palm for the dead. Last of all comes the Poppy panel, representing the fourth gold of California.

Ben Macomber

"The entire scheme - the conception and birth of Art, its commitment to the earth, its progress and acceptance by the human intellect, - is expressed in the four major panels. They are lighted from below by a brilliant flood of golden light, the sunshine of California, and reach up into the intense blue of the California skies." This, as well as much of the interpretation of the eight pictures, is drawn from Reid's own account.

Within the rotunda has been installed Paul Wayland Bartlett's spirited equestrian statue of Lafayette. This is a replica of the original work, which was presented to the French Government by the school children of the United States, and stands in the gardens of the Louvre. Other notable statues here are Karl Bitter's Thomas Jefferson, John J. Boyle's Commodore Barry, Herbert Adams's Bryant, and Robert T. McKenzie's charming figure of "The Young Franklin." Outside the rotunda, facing the main entrance to the gallery, is "The Pioneer Mother," Charles Grafly, sculptor. Over the entrance is Leo Lentelli's "Aspiration."

Beautiful as is the Palace of Fine Arts by day, it is even more lovely at night. (p. 137.) Either by moonlight or under the gentle flood of illumination that rests softly upon it when the heavens are dark, it is wonderful. There is so much of perfection in the building, and it is so well placed, that it needs no special conditions to be at its best. Nor is any particular viewpoint necessary. Stand where you will around this structure, or on the opposite margin of the lagoon, and each position gives you a different grouping of columns and dome and wall, a different setting of trees and water. The form of the Palace is responsible for this. Roughly speaking, a rectangular structure presents but four views. But the great arc of the Fine Arts, with its detached colonnade following the same curve on either side of the rotunda, is not so restricted. Every new point of view discloses new beauty. The breadth of the lagoon before it guarantees a proper perspective. It is impossible not to see it aright.

An excellent test of the quality of all such temporary structures is the satisfaction with which one thinks of them as permanent buildings. No other of the palaces would wear so well in its beauty if it were set up for the joy of future generations. It would be a glorious thing for San Francisco if the Fine Arts Palace could be made permanent in Golden Gate Park. To duplicate it in lasting materials would cost much, but it would be worth while. San Francisco owes it to itself and its love for art to see that this greatest of Western works of art does not pass away. As it stands on the Exposition grounds, it is more enduring than any of the other palaces. To induce the loan of its priceless contents, the building had to be fireproof. But the construction is not permanent. The splendid colonnade, a thing of exquisite and manifold beauty, is only plaster, and can last but a season or two. Even were the building solid enough to endure, its location is impossible after the Exposition closes.

It should be duplicated in permanent form. No doubt a proper site, with a setting of water and trees, can best be found in Golden Gate Park. The steel frame and roof of the main gallery could easily be transferred there and set up again. While it would cost too much to duplicate in real marble the pillars of the colonnade and dome, yet these can be reproduced in artificial stone as successfully as they have here been imitated in plaster. In the Pennsylvania Railroad station in New

York travertine has been counterfeited so well that no one can tell where the real ends and the imitation begins.

Every other considerable city in the civilized world has its art gallery. San Francisco has already the full-sized model of surely the most beautiful one in the world. Made permanent in the Park, this Palace of Art would not only honor San Francisco, but would be "a joy forever" to all America.

The Fine Arts Exhibit[1]. - The Palace of Fine Arts contains what the International Jury declares the best and most important collection of modern art that has yet been assembled in America. The war in Europe had a two-fold effect on this exhibition. While it prevented some countries, like Russia and Germany, from sending their paintings and sculptures, it led others, such as France and Italy, to send more than they otherwise would have sent. The number the Exposition might have was limited only by its funds available for insurance. So many were the works of art sent over on the Vega and the Jason that an Annex was required to house them.

It must be remembered that this art exhibit, like the other exhibits of the Exposition, is contemporaneous. It represents, with exceptions, the work of the last decade. Most of the exceptions are in the rooms of the Historical Section, the Abbey, Sargent, Whistler, Keith, and other loan collections, and the great Chinese exhibit of ancient paintings on silk. In general, the paintings and sculptures made famous by time are not in the Fine Arts Palace. Its rooms are mainly filled with the latest work of artists of the day, exhibited under the Exposition's rule which limits competition in all departments to current production. This explains, for instance, why the French Government has placed its Meissoniers and Detailles, with Rodin's bronzes, in the French Pavilion. A Michelangelo, works of Benvenuto Cellini, and many old paintings and statues are in the beautiful Italian Pavilion. Other paintings of value are in the Belgian section of the French Pavilion, and in the Danish Pavilion.

This limitation of the Fine Arts exhibit has made room for a great representation of the men of today. The Palace contains a multitude of splendid pictures. While of course, as in all such collections, there is some inferior work, the most pertinent criticism is that there are too many really notable things, and the scope of the collection is too broad, to be seen with due appreciation in a limited time. There is so liberal a showing of different schools, styles and lands, that one is liable at first to be bewildered. But the exhibit is most popular. The great number of visitors constantly thronging the galleries is significant of the value the people put upon art. Excellent as the collection is as a school for artists, it was made for popular enjoyment and education. The best result to be looked for is its stimulation and culture of the public taste. The people are already in love with it, and what they love they make their own.

The exhibits are arranged in fifteen sections, consisting of national, sectional, or personal, collections of paintings, besides many important displays of miniatures, etchings, prints, drawings, and tapestries. The art of the sculptor is abundantly illustrated in grouped statuary, single pieces, panels in low or high relief, and wood carvings. Passing the heroic emblems of history or allegory in marble, bronze or plaster, nothing is more

Ben Macomber

beautiful or appealing than the hundreds of small bronzes shown. In brief, the Fine Arts exhibit embraces all the classifications of modern art, save the "arts and crafts" exhibits, which are scattered among the several exhibit palaces.

First in importance to a citizen of this country is the art of the United States. Possibly it may also be of first importance to foreign visitors. For the phrase "American art" no longer raises a doubt. It is at last recognized that America has something of its own to offer the world, - a style developed within the last, two decades. The prime movement of the times presenting boldness, brilliance and a laxity of detail in portrayal, the art of America, as shown in this exhibition, embodies these characteristics without emphasizing them. Keeping in mind the fact that the Palace contains little American art earlier than 1905, American artists are showing marked individualities, even in their acceptance of popular precepts. The virile men of the day love luminosity; it dominates all else, and marks their canvases with light; they restrain the too bold stroke of the radical Impressionist, but outline with firmness, so that details are more easily imagined by the observer, even when an expected delineation is absent. Even the older men, though still under the influence of earlier tradition, show a distinctiveness of style that sets them well apart from their English, French or German contemporaries.

The International Section, in Room 108 and in the Annex, is peculiarly interesting in that it makes easy a comparison of the characteristic fingerprints of each country represented. There is ample opportunity here for a discriminating and profitable study. Unfortunately, because of the war, the gallery contains no special rooms for the art of England and Germany. Both countries are represented only by loan collections. Of German art there are forty well chosen paintings.

France, Italy, Holland, Sweden, Portugal, Japan, China and several of the South American countries have installed representative collections in the Palace; while the Annex, made necessary by the unexpected number of pictures from Europe, contains a large exhibit of Hungarian art, a Norwegian display, filling seven rooms, a large British exhibit, and a small group of pictures by Spanish painters, showing that the influence of Velasquez is still powerful in Spanish art. The Norwegian display is one of the largest foreign sections, quite as characteristic as the Swedish, and certain to arouse discussion because of its extreme modernism. The ultra-radical art of Edvard Munch, who is called the greatest of Norwegian painters, and to whom a special room is assigned, is sure to be a bone of contention among the critics. The work of Harald Sohlberg (medal of honor) and Halfdan Strom (gold medal), differing widely from Munch's, though hardly less modern in style, will also attract much attention. The omission of Munch from the honor list is really a tribute to his eminence. An artist who has won the Grand Prix at Rome and awards in every other European capital was deemed outside of competition here.

Axel Gallen-Kallela, the celebrated Finnish painter, winner of the Exposition's medal of honor, fills another room in the Annex. This room, covering adequately Gallen's progress through twenty-five years, is the only one in the Exposition to illustrate the development of a great painter from his student days. The collection runs

Ben Macomber

from his earliest academic work, photographic in its care for detail, to his present mastery of Impressionism, wherein by a few strokes he expresses all the essentials.

The Italian Futurists are well shown in the Annex, and for the first time in this country. The Futurist pictures hitherto seen in America have been French imitations of the Italian originators of the mode. A sample Futurist title, "Architectural Construction of a Woman on the Beach," may or may not indicate what these pictures reveal. The Annex, too, has a splendid exhibit of the etchings of Frank Brangwyn, the great Englishman, who is no less renowned as an etcher than as a painter, and who has won the Exposition's medal of honor in the International Section.

The arrangement of the rooms in the Fine Arts Gallery becomes simple enough when the key is supplied. The United States section is in the center, and, with the historical rooms, occupies, roughly, half the space, flanked by the foreign rooms at either end of the building. Four rooms of the United States section are separated from the rest and form a narrow strip across the extreme north end of the gallery. The prints, drawings, miniatures, and medals are installed in rooms forming a strip along the west wall of the building.

The United States section is opened by a central hall opposite the main entrance, and by a corridor extending on either side through to the foreign sections. The central hall is chiefly devoted to sculpture, including Karl Bitter's strong and character-istic group, "The Signing of the Louisiana Purchase Treaty," Daniel Chester French's "Alice Freeman Palmer Memorial," both winners of the medal of honor, Gertrude Vanderbilt Whitney's fine central fountain, and other important work. The walls are hung with ancient tapestries of great interest, and paintings, mostly decorative, though Robert Vonnoh's "Poppies" and Ben Au Haggin's "Little White Dancer" are admirable. Vonnoh won a gold medal.

Historical Section. - South of the United States section, a block of ten rooms, with Room 54 at the southwest angle of the central hall, is devoted to painters who either have influenced American art or represent its earlier stages. Room 91, on the east side of the block, contains old Dutch, Flemish, French, and Italian pictures, none very interesting, though Teniers, Watteau and Tintoretto are represented. Rooms 92, 62, and 61, constituting the tier next to the Italian section, show chiefly examples of the French painters, including those of the Barbizon school, who have influenced later American painting. Along with other names less known, Room 92 displays canvases by Daubigny, Courbet, Charles Le Brun, Meissonier, Tissot, Monticelli and Rousseau. It has two Corots, one a delight. Room 62 is even more important. It offers a Millet, far from typical; a capital Schreyer, two portraits by the German Von Lenbach, a small but interesting sample of Alma Tadema's finished style, and the sensational "Consolatrix Afflictorum" by Dagnan-Bouveret. Better still, in Jules Breton's "The Vintage" and Troyon's "Landscape and Cattle" it has two of the noblest paintings to be seen in the entire Palace, - pictures that show these great masters at their best.

Room 61 is mainly devoted to the early Impressionists, with seven canvases by their leader, Claude Monet,

Ben Macomber

and other landscapes by Renoir, Pissaro and Sisley, and a brilliant interior (No. 2343) by Gaston La Touche. The pictures by Monet illustrate his progress from the hard conventionalism of his early academic style (seen in 2636) to such delightful embodiments of light and atmosphere as 2633 and 2637. The gallery contains no more triumphant piece of Impressionism than the saucy "Lady in Pink" by the Russian, Nicholas Fechin. The story set afloat that it is the work of an untaught Russian peasant simply testifies to ignorance of this master. Every splotch of color here breathes technique. As if by way of contrast, the opposite wall shows one of Puvis de Chavannes' classical murals, even more anaemic than usual.

The large room No. 63 shows a Venetian sunset by Turner, two portraits by Goya, another attributed to Velasquez, a splendid Raffaelesque altar-piece by Tiepolo, the like of which rarely leaves Italy, and canvases by Guido Reni, Ribera, and Van Dyke. Almost all the remaining space is taken up by excellent examples of the British art that influenced the early American painters, with some of prior date. Here are canvases by Lely, Kneller, Hogarth, Reynolds, Gainsborough, Hoppner, Beechey, Allan Ramsay, Lawrence, Raeburn, and Romney. The last four are especially well represented. In this room, too, is the bronze replica of Weinmann's figure, "The Setting Sun," here called "Descending Night."

American "Old Masters." - Following logically the English portrait painters, the American historical section begins with Rooms 60 and 59. The former is mainly filled with the work, much of it admirable, of the early American portrait painters. Here are Gilbert Stuart's lovable "President Monroe," Benjamin West's

"Magdalen," and portraits by Peale, Copley, West, Sully and others. In Room 59, the antiquarian interest predominates, with a few fine portraits by Inman, Harding, King, and S. F. B. Morse, who, besides inventor, was an artist. But nothing here surpasses No. 1719 by Charles Loring Elliott, a canvas that is irresistible in its vivid setting forth of personality. Room 58 brings the story of American painting well past the middle of the Nineteenth century, with typical examples of Bierstadt, Eastman Johnson and other fading names. Room 57 contains a number of Edwin Abbey's finely illustrative paintings, the most popular of which is his "Penance of Eleanor," and a collection of his splendid drawings; also important canvases by Theodore Robinson and John La Farge. Room 64 covers a wide sweep, from Church's archaic "Niagara Falls" down to Stephen Parrish, Eakins, Martin, the Morans, Hovenden, and Remington. Edward Moran's "Brush Burning" (2649) is capital. Room 54, the last of the American historical rooms, is perhaps the most important, finely showing Inness, Wyant, Winslow Homer, Hunt, and other American masters.

Modern American Painting. - We come now to the great and splendid representation of present-day painters. In noting these, the artists achieving grand prizes, medals of honor or gold medals will often be mentioned; but a full list of such honors will be found at the end of this chapter. It should be remembered that no member of a jury, and no man who received the honor of a separate room, was eligible for award. In general, it may be said, the Exposition puts forward the work of artists who have "arrived" since the opening of the century. In accordance with this helpful policy, older painters who had won many honors at previous exhibitions were passed over for the encouragement of younger men. It should also be noted that awards were not made for particular pictures, but upon each artist's exhibit as a whole.

Rooms 55, 56, 65 and 85 show contemporary Americans, - the last two with great credit. No. 65 is a large room of canvases by American women painters. One who has not kept abreast of woman's work in art in this country has a surprise awaiting him in the the high quality shown here. Two pictures by Ellen Rand (2919, 2918), Mary Curtis Richardson's captivating "Young Mother" and her "Professor Paget" (3000, 3002), and Alice Stoddard's inimitably girlish group, "The Sisters" (3329), will reward very careful study of their sincerity and strength of treatment. Especially brilliant are the works of Cecilia Beaux and M. Jean McLane, - the first winning the Exposition's medal of honor, the latter rather theatrical in their gayety of color. Here also is a canvas (2743) by Violet Oakley, another honor medallist.

Room 85 is enriched by the canvases of Charles Walter Stetson, Horatio Walker, Charles W. Hawthorne, Douglas Volk (gold medal), and George de Forest Brush. Volk's three charming pictures deserve to be better hung. The Stetson group illustrates the Impressionist method and result as well as anything in the Palace. Take his "Smugglers" or his "Summer Joy" (3311, 3317), and note how a few heavy and apparently meaningless dabs of color may be laid side by side on canvas in such a way that, when seen from a distance, they blend, until the picture not only outlines figures and foliage, but also glows with atmosphere, life and movement.

These rooms complete the south half of the American

section, with the exception of the very interesting, though not fully adequate, Whistler Room, 28; the Print Rooms, 29 to 34, in the tier along the west wall, and five more one-man rooms along the east wall. These five, in their order from the main entrance are: No. 87, devoted to the old-masterlike works of Frank Duveneck, who, more perhaps than any other American, shows the great manner of Velasquez, Rembrandt and Franz Hals, and to whom the jury has recommended that a special medal be given for his influence on American art; No. 88 filled with the admirable Impressionist landscapes of E. W. Redfield; 89 and 93, given up to the widely contrasted work of Edmund C. Tarbell and John H. Twachtman, each in his own fashion a master and enjoying a well-earned popularity, Twachtman's pictures in particular commanding almost as high prices as those of the men in Room 54; and No. 90, just off the Tarbell room, containing a small loan collection which very incompletely represents William Keith. Five other individual rooms are north of the main entrance: No. 79, portraits and still life by William M. Chase; 78, Childe Hassam's radically Impressionist work; 77, Gari Melchers' pictures of Dutch types and scenes; 76, the charming western pictures of Arthur F. Mathews and Francis McComas, both Californians; and 75, the John S. Sargent room, containing among other works his famous early portrait of Mme. Gautrin, his "John Hay," and the sympathetic portrait of Henry James which was mutilated by the British suffragettes. All these one-man rooms exhibit characteristic work of the men thus distinguished, though the younger men are the more completely represented. The Whistler, Keith, Chase and Sargent rooms, which may be classed with the historical block, show few of the best-known masterpieces of these artists.

Ben Macomber

Room 80, cut out of the northeast corner of the central hall, a gallery of well restrained pictures, contains the interesting work in light and color of William McG. Paxton, member of the jury; portraits and figures by Leslie P. Thompson (silver medal), Philip L. Hale's warm-toned portraits, the delicate but brilliant landscapes of Willard L. Metcalf (medal of honor), and those by Philip Little (silver medal). The portraits are in the older academic style; the landscapes, modern. Rooms 67 and 68 are distinguished by some notable landscapes and marines. No. 67 shows Emil Carlsen's fresh "Open Sea," his single picture here, but the winner of a medal of honor, and Albert Laessle's small animal sculptures (gold medal), and capital examples of Paul Dougherty, J. F. Carlson, Leonard Ochtman and Ben Foster. No. 68 holds two fine snowy landscapes by W. Elmer Schofield (medal of honor), two engaging studies in brown by Daniel Garber, brilliant figures by J. C. Johansen, and California coast views by William Ritschel. The last three artists are gold medallists.

Room 69 is made noteworthy by works of three of the nine American winners of the medal of honor, - Lawton Parker's voluptuous "Paresse" and two portraits, and single paintings by John W. Alexander and Richard E. Miller (1035, 2606). Alexander's airy "Phyllis" is his only picture in the Palace. Miller shows one more canvas, a colorful "Nude" (2607) in Room 47. Room 70 is entirely devoted to portrait painters, among them Julian Story, H. G. Herkomer, Robert Vonnoh, and Irving C. Wiles (3668), the latter two both winners of the gold medal. No. 74 shows admirable small landscapes, among them the "Group of White Birches" by Will S. Robinson (silver medal), Charles C. Allen's "Mountain and Cloud," and land

and water views by Charles J. Taylor, especially No. 3404. Room 73 shows good landscapes by Ernest Lawson (gold medal), Paul King (silver medal), and the two Beals. Gifford Beal's work won a gold medal. Room 72, a gallery in the academic style, contains a variety of portraits, figure paintings and landscapes, including W. R. Leigh's spirited "Stampede," and the more conventional work of Walter MacEwen. No. 71 is another varied room. In addition to some landscapes, the visitor will be struck by the small but exquisite exhibit in gold, enamel, and precious stones of Louis C. Tiffany.

The western tier of this section, Rooms 43-51, contains work of all grades of merit. No. 43 is conglomerate. Perham Nahl's well drawn "Despair" (2690) is perhaps best worth mention. In No. 44 Putthuff's two brown western scenes and Clarkson's portrait of E. G. Keith are interesting. No. 45 is better. Walter Griffin's opulent landscapes (medal of honor) are well worth studying. Here also are two canvases by Robert Reid, one almost Japanese in its effect; the restrained landscapes of William Sartain, and Charles Morris Young's sharply contrasting "Red Mill' and "Gray Mill," with his characteristic wintry landscapes. Reid and Young won the gold medal. In No. 46 are a half-dozen delicately handled landscapes by Frank V. Du Mond, a member of the jury. In No. 47 E. L. Blumenschein's warm Indian pictures and A. L. Groll's desert scenes won silver medals. But the best thing here is Richard E. Miller's "Nude," already mentioned.

On the east wall of Room 48 hangs "Sleep," the best of the eight canvases shown by Frederic Carl Frieseke, distinguished above all other American painters in the palace by the Exposition's grand prize. Seven other

Ben Macomber

pictures by Frieseke, interesting by reason of comparison with this masterpiece, hang in Room 117. In Gallery 48 are also some good landscapes, - Robert Vonnoh's "Bridge at Grez" and Cullen Yates' "November Snow." In No. 49, a better balanced room than most in this tier, three walls are made noteworthy by J. Alden Weir's luminous and Impressionist landscapes, and D. W. Tryon's more academic canvases. Weir was the chairman of the jury for oil paintings. No. 50 is dominated by Sergeant Kendall, in both painting and sculpture. In the first he won the gold medal, in the second the silver medal. Room 51 has been called the "Chamber of Horrors," because it shows several of the extremists; but it has some masterpieces. Staring things by John Sloan, William J. Glackens, Adolphe Borie, and Arthur B. Caries are relieved by H. H. Breckinridge's highly colored fruits and flowers, Gertrude Lampert's "Black and Green," Thomas Anshutz' two studies of women, and several of Robert Henri's strong figure pieces.

In the extreme northern end of the gallery, beyond the foreign sections, is a tier of four rooms, 117-120, ranging from the mediocre to the admirable. In No. 117 are seven interesting canvases by Frieseke, the grand-prize winner, already mentioned. These pictures show the artist's scope. No. 1816 and others are strikingly like Plinio Nomellini's No. 86 in the Italian section. No. 1811 is as different from these as "Sleep" is from all the rest. In the same room are Mora's "Vacation Time" (2645) and Tanner's "Christ at the Home of Lazarus" (3370), both winners of the gold medal. Room 118 holds the pictures of several gold-medal winners, the "Promenade" (1185) by Max Bohm; the noble "Lake Louise" (1246) by H. J. Breuer, whose pictures of the Canadian Rockies are also to be found in Rooms 56 and 58; the tender "Spring" (1972) by W. D. Hamilton, worthy of a better place; and H. L. Hoffman's clearlighted "A Mood of Spring" (2116), and his vivid "Savannah Market" (2115).

Room 119 is filled with water-colors, drawings, engravings and etchings. Room 120 holds George Bellows' Post-Impressionistic canvases, Myron Barlow's well-drawn figures, W. D. Hamilton's speaking likeness of Justice McKenna (1971), Charles H. Woodbury's "The Bark" (3692), and Waldo Murray's portrait of "Robert Fowler" (366), wrongly catalogued with the International section. All these painters won gold medals. This is perhaps the best room in this tier.

In the tier on the western wall devoted to the minor forms of art, Howard Pyle's illustrations occupy two small rooms, 41 and 42. The first contains ink sketches, the second his works in characteristic color. Room 40 is devoted to admirable miniatures and to water colors. Here on the east wall are Jules Guerin's vividly colored Oriental scenes, which won the gold medal. The walls of Room 39 are given up to a series of charming pastels by John McClure Hamilton. No. 39 also contains cases of medals, as does No. 38. Room 37 is devoted to miniatures, and 36 to drawings.

In the section known as the "Print Rooms," 29-34, along the west wall, are hundreds of famous etchings. This branch of art, old and respected through the examples offered by early masters like Albrecht Durer and Rembrandt, has still to be fully appreciated. It has come to the public slowly, the layman who likes and buys pictures more often holding aloof from the thing

Ben Macomber

called an etching. That there is now a closer acquaintance than before is due in large measure to Joseph Pennell. Working through the practical, he allied his art years ago with such subjects as bridge and railroad building, and by giving the public an easier avenue of approach, has attracted it to the beauty of this method of art. The print rooms show dozens of Pennell's etchings, with those of Whistler and many others. Whistler's etchings, lithographs, and drawings are in No. 29, Pennell's in No. 31. Room 30 holds the work of Henry Wolf, winner of the grand prize. B. A. Wehrschmidt, an honor medallist, is represented in Room 119. J. Andre Smith, Herman A. Webster and Cadwallader Washburn are in Room 32, Allen Lewis and Gustav Baumann (gold medals) are in Room 34. Room 28 holds the loan collection of Whistler's works, already mentioned, chiefly from the National Gallery, Washington. Room 27 contains photographic reproductions of painting and sculpture. Room 26 is devoted to original drawings for illustration.

The Foreign Sections. - These are placed north and south of the United States collections. In the extreme south end, Japan occupies a large block of rooms, numbered from 1 to 10. With this abundant floor and wall space at her disposal, that country left nothing undone to make her art exhibit comprehensive and beautiful. The display stands alone for completeness. Japan's art is as old as her history; and now, with her advent among the modern nations, she has added Occidental art to her more ancient forms. The essayal, as shown here, is still beyond her, but the strides are noteworthy. In the wonderful display of her own art, she shows both the beauties of antiquity and the masterpieces of her present day artists. The paintings upon silk, landscape embroideries, porcelains, ink drawings, metal work, and scrolls will occupy the art lover many hours.

France adjoins Japan, filling a block of rooms from 12 to 18, and Italy follows, in Rooms 21 to 25. The intervening rooms, Nos. 19 and 20, are assigned respectively to Uruguay and Cuba.

The French and Italian exhibits had to wait for the arrival of the Jason. Now they are installed, and beautifully hung and set. Though France is the home of the Post-Impressionists, and Italy that of the Futurists, the flagrancy of neither of these schools is on view here. Both countries show their best balanced art since 1905. In the French exhibit, the mode of the day prevails, color, luminosity, richness of texture. All that differentiates the art of France to-day from that of other countries is her own inimitable, delicate, inherent taste and touch. The subject matters little; the French perception and execution are there. Where other canvases offer - say a beautiful glow - the French picture "vibrates." If other works are finished, these have finesse. There is similar spirit in the Italian galleries, with a variation due to national characteristics rather than to difference of opinion or method. The Italian pictures fully occupy the mind and eye; the French often fascinate by something more than skill and color. Both countries have placed their older art, and some of its best, in their official pavilions.

France. - In the French Section, Room 12 contains a diverse collection of water color, drawing, engraving, and painting, among the latter, Henry Grosjean's "The Bottoms" (365). Room 13, full of strongly contrasting work, is distinguished by Maurice Denis' daring decorative panels. Here also is Claude Monet's

"Vetheuil" (452), the same scene, though not the same picture, as his No. 2634 in Room 61. Comparison is interesting for the difference in touch, though both were painted in the same year. Francois Flameng is represented here by "Paris" (346), not so compelling as his "Madame Letellier" (345), and "Fete Venetienne" (344), in Rooms 18 and 14. Room 14, containing a good many decorative canvases, has also, besides Flameng's "Fete," two of the extreme Impressionistic paintings of Henri Martin, "The Lovers" (432), and his own dim "Self Portrait" (433). Two colorful Breton scenes (302) by Darrieux, and (406) by Le Gout-Gerard stand out on the north wall. Room 15 shows some charming pieces, - Lucien Simon's strongly contrasting work in the spiritual "Communicants" (494) and his barbaric "Gondola" (495); Domergue's "The Frog" (324), Besnard's glowing "Gipsy" (255), and Lemordant's "The Wind" (409). These last give a strong color to the room, relieved by Leroux' calm "Lake" (416), and Maury's delicate young girls (440).

Room 16 is better balanced. Remembering "The Frog," Domergue's versatility appears in the portrait of Gina Mabille, the danseuse. A delicate bit of Impressionism in Le Sidanier's "The Harbor: Landernau" (418). Two canvases by Menard are hung here. His "Opal Sea" (445) is charming. Auburtin's decorative panels hang on the north wall. One of the most notable works of P. Franc Lamy, his golden "Venice: Morning" (393), will be found on the west wall.

Room 17 shows little of striking interest. Augustin Hanicotte, one of the few French painters to adopt the strong colors and lights of the Scandinavian artists, is represented by the gay "Winter in the Low Country" (381). Andre Dauchez' "Le Pouldu" (304) is a fine brown lowland landscape. In spirit, though in richer colors, Jean Veber's captivating "Little Princess" (515) reminds one of John Bauer's Swedish fairy-tale pictures. Strength and truthfulness characterize Jeanniot's fine group of Norman fisherfolk (388). (See p. 125.)

Room 18 is better. Note Marie Cazin's "Diana Asleep" (289), done in a single brown. Here, too, is Flameng's "Portrait of Madame Letellier" (345). A soft, delicate bit of landscape is Brouillet's "Among the Dunes" (272), which deserves better than to be hung in a corner. One who has seen the Futurist pictures in the Annex should not overlook here Albert Guillaume's "Le Boniment" (370), a rich burlesque on Futurist art.

Italy. - No other section in the Palace is so finely hung as the Italian. As no attempt has been made to crowd the rooms, each canvas is properly placed. Room 21 holds the most important paintings honored by the jury. On the west wall is the work of Ettore Tito, the winner of the grand prize, five canvases demonstrating both his versatility and his mastery of color. On the north and south walls are the medal-of-honor pictures of Onorato Carlandi and Camillo Innocenti, the latter striking in their golden tone. Coromaldi's rich harvest scenes (26, 27), and a Leonardo Bazzaro (4) (both gold medallists), hang on the east wall. Not to be overlooked, though passed by the jury, are Casciaro's warm landscapes on the north wall and Ricci's "Butterflies" (96), which help to make this collection one of splendid color.

Room 22 also glows with color. Ferraguti's "Portrait in Red" (46) (gold medal) holds the place of honor on the west wall. On the north wall is the glowing "Fiametta"

Ben Macomber

(49) by Matilde Festa Piacentini, wife of the architect of the Italian Pavilion, and beside it the equally warm "Golden Rays" (47) by Ferretti. On the east wall burns Traiano Chitarin's "Evening Fires" (31). Among the sculpture is Dazzi's "Portrait of a Lady" (160) (gold medal).

Room 23 holds the greater portion of the sculpture, including Amigoni's simple "Adolescence" (151), Brozzi's spirited "Animals" (155), in relievo on bronze, Graziosi's "Susanna" (165), and Pagliani's "On the Beach" (180). All of these won gold medals, but the really striking piece in the room is "Proximus Tuus" (162), the weary peasant, by Achille D'Orsi. Of the few paintings nothing is very remarkable, though Bazzani's "Arch of Septimus Severus" (3) is interesting for its workmanship.

Room 24 presents extremely varied styles from Morani's No. 80 to Domenico Irolli's heavily painted "Violin Player" (64), and Enrico Lionne's gorgeous purple figures in the extreme of Impressionism. One of Nomellini's effects in light and shade appears in No. 86, on the east wall. Paolo Sala's "Along the Thames" (100) deserves better place and notice. Irolli, Lionne and Nomellini are gold medallists.

Room 25, without any remarkable canvases, is very pleasing as an example of harmonious hanging. This is best illustrated by the west wall where hang four pictures by the three Ciardis, Beppe, Emma, and Guiseppe, and one, No. 6, by Bartolomeo Bezzi, the group admirably centered by Beppe Ciardi's large "Venetian Scene" (32). All three of the Ciardis won gold medals. In the center of the north wall is a fine ruddy sunset (102) by Francesco Sartorelli. The south wall is dominated by Z. V. Zanetti's richly decorative "Tree" (116). Beside it, on the cut-off of the wall, is Guiseppe Mentessi's gripping "Soul of the Stones" (75). Mentessi won the gold medal with this picture, as Italo Brass did with his "Bridge Across the Lagoon" (10). Sculpture in this room is represented by small bronzes and Ernesto Biondi's almost terrible "St. Francis d'Assisi" (154).

Uruguay. - The Uruguayan exhibit of painting and sculpture is in one small room, No. 19, against the west wall, next to France. The work has characteristics in common with that of the south of Europe, and shows national feeling. Manuel Rose (52-57) was awarded a gold medal.

Cuba. - The Cuban section in Room 20, adjoining Uruguay, though small, is interesting. The jury thought well enough of Leopoldo Romanach's canvases (16-29) to give him the medal of honor. M. Rodriguez Morey (13-15) won the gold medal.

China, occupying four rooms, 94-97, adjoining the northern end of the United States Section, though desirous of appearing before the world as a modern republic, has wisely brought here the most beautiful examples of her ancient art. Many of the pieces go so far beyond the records of man that their authorship is lost in darkness. The exquisitely beautiful ink paintings on silk, the finest collection of these works in existence, represent the master painters of all the dynasties of China. Their subjects deal with tradition and religious precepts. Precious cloisonne in heroic pieces has been used for the background of paintings. There are picture-screens made of five or six attached panels of fine porcelain inlaid with cloisonne, and many splendid carvings and porcelains. The medal of honor for water color went to Kiang Ying-seng's "Snow Scene" (348) in Room 94. The water colors of Su Chen-lien, Kao Ki-fong, and Miss Shin Ying-chin, and the exquisite carvings in semi-precious stones of Teh Chang, all gold medal winners, are in the same room.

The Philippines, Room 98, by the west wall, have an exhibit which shows that their march toward civilization includes well-grounded ambitions of art. Mentality, feeling, spirit, all reveal themselves in the canvases. Crudity is apparent, but it comes more from an untutored hand than from failure to grasp the significance of the subject. Many pictures are flamboyant, some are melodramatic, nearly all are big subjects handled with great boldness; what they lack in finish they make up in sincerity. Felix R. Hidalgo's contributions (10-20) won him a gold medal.

Sweden. - The achievements of Sweden, Rooms 99-107, next to China, have surprised everybody. That country has sent the most distinctively national of all the European exhibits. Swedish artists are stay-at-homes, and their pictures are filled with the Scandinavian love of country. The scenes and portraits are all Swedish, from Carl Larsson's intimate pictures of family life and forest picnics (see p. 126), or Bruno Liljefors' great paintings of the misty northern ocean, down to John Bauer's captivating little illustrations of Swedish goblin tales. No one who has viewed the snow scenes of Anshelm Schultzberg can ever forget the impression of cold and impenetrable depth. Swedish painters are heroic in method, very lavish with their pigments, and generous in the size of their canvases. Some of the pictures, in fact, like "The

Swans" (202) by Liljefors, are too large to be seen to the best advantage in the small rooms where they hang. Liljefors won the grand prize, and Gustav Fjaestad the medal of honor, for Swedish painting; Larsson, the grand prize for water color. Anna Boberg, Room 106, whose masculine paintings have always won her honor hitherto, is without award. This famous painter is the wife of the architect of the fine Swedish Pavilion. The jury offered her a silver medal, but Commissioner Schultzberg refused to accept it.

Spain is to have an excellent exhibit in the Annex building behind the Palace. Thus far Portugal alone represents the Iberian painters. The collection fills three rooms, 109-111, between Sweden and Holland. The Portuguese artists infuse the spirit of revelry into much of their work. Indeed, it sometimes approaches the bacchanalian. The work is of the extreme modern school as to color, although, technically, there is much drawing in and respect for definite form. Most striking, perhaps, is the splendid representation in many of the pictures of the intense sunlight that beats upon that Southern country. No more vivid examples of this can be found in the collection than Malhoa's "Returning from the Festival" (54) and his "Catholic Procession in the Country" (56). Malhoa, deservedly, captured the grand prize for Portuguese art. The single medal of honor went to Jose Veloso Salgado for his scenes of Minho. The portraits, too, have much of the intensity of the South. The most noteworthy are those by Columbano, Room 110, winner of the grand prize at St. Louis. The four rooms show Portugal prolific of artists who seek beauty in scenes of domesticity and the qrandeur of landscapes.

Argentina. - It is interesting to note that the painters of

Portugal show more characteristics in common with those of South America and the Philippines than with their European neighbors. Their execution is more tamed than that of the Filipino painters, their style more settled than that of the Argentine. That is not to the discredit of the Argentinos, who, though a new people, have accomplished much that deserves praise. Their exhibit, in Room 112, is important in its showing of the progress of art in so new a country, and it is said to be representative. The artists whose works are shown are almost all young men, a fact which, in connection with their performance, proclaims that Argentina will do something free and original in the future. Three pictures by Antonio Alice, Nos. 1, 2, and 3, have been awarded the medal of honor. They bear witness to Alice's great versatility. Jorge Bermudez' three figure studies (gold medal) are striking. No. 5, "The Daughter of the Hacienda," is wrongly entitled in the official catalog "The Young Landlady." Others in the collection suffer in the same way, as Coppini's "The Old Station" (20), which is catalogued as "The Old Stall." Some of the Argentino landscapes are striking expositions of the spirit of the pampas, particularly Lavecchia's "Near Twilight" (35). As a whole, the paintings are significant of the country of their painters, a truly worthy quality. The sculpture in this room, particularly "Increase and Multiply" (75), by Pedro Zonza Briano (medal of honor), and a splendid Indian portrait (32), by Alberto Lagos (gold medal), is admirable.

The International Room, No. 108, on the east wall between Sweden, Holland and Portugal, contains but a small portion of the foreign pictures. Its chief feature is the exhibit of German art. Franz Stuck's "Summer Night" (459), Heinrich von Zugel's "In the Rhine

Meadows" (549), both winners of the medal of honor; Curt Agthe's "At the Spring" (3), and Leo Putz' "The Shore" (387), gold-medal pictures, are worthily characteristic of Germany's best art. "El Cristo de los Andes," by E. W. Christmas (bronze medal) is interesting. The bulk of the pictures under "International Section" are in the Annex.

Holland, in Rooms 113-116, shows an art so different in its characteristics from that of Sweden that she might be at the other end of the earth. Where the Swedish artists show boldness, sometimes almost to the point of crudeness, the Dutch are intent on some degree of finish. Modernity of color is apparent, and while there are few strokes that indicate timidity, there are fine touches of the poetic in which the Hollander's heart shows its love of home and gardens. Those great tulip beds are real and luscious. Family life in the Netherlands is shown in several fine interiors, and the portraits by Dutch artists are more graceful than those of the average modernist. The grand prize in the Netherlands section went to Breitner's snowy "Amsterdam Timber Port" (17). Bauer's "Oriental Equestrian" (7) won the medal of honor. Gold medals were given to seven artists, named in the list following this chapter.

A thoroughly delightful portion of the art exhibit is the sculpture shown in the colonnades and on the grounds of the Palace. This is the first time a great exhibit has been displayed in such a manner. It adds everything to the effectiveness of the sculpture, wherever the pieces have been designed to be erected out of doors. It has been possible to show much of the fountain sculpture in its actual relation to real fountains, and to give the hunters and Indians, the nymphs and the satyrs, the

Ben Macomber

advantage of natural backgrounds. In addition to the contemporaneous sculpture there are some famous pieces here, such as Saint-Gaudens' Lincoln, brought from Chicago, and the copy of Bartlett's equestrian Lafayette. Among recent sculpture, one of the most interesting works shown is a group by C. L. Pietro, of New York, "The Mother of the Dead," - a powerful story in bronze of the burden which the war has brought to woman. (See p. 120.) Pietro's modeling is worthy of an older artist. Another human tragedy is well told in "The Outcast," a graphic figure by Attilio Piccirilli. (p. 136.) Charming bits of comedy are the whimsical little fountain pieces by Janet Scudder and Anna Coleman Ladd. The honor-winners in sculpture are named in the following list.

Awards

Awards have been completed and announced by the Fine Arts juries in all sections except the French. The following list includes all the grand prizes, medals of honor and gold medals. The numerous silver and bronze medals and honorable mentions are omitted. Numbers following the names indicate the rooms where the work may be found.

United States Section. -

Oil Painting

Grand Prize. - F. C. Frieseke, 48, 117.

Medals of Honor. - John W. Alexander, 69; Cecilia Beaux, 65; Emil Carlsen. 67; Walter Griffin, 45; Violet

Oakley, 65; Willard L. Metcalf, 80; Richard E. Miller, 47, 69; Lawton Parker, 69; W. E. Schofield, 68.

Gold Medals. - Myron Barlow. 120; Gifford Beal, 73; George Bellows, 120; Max Bohm, 72, 118; H. H. Breckenridge, 51; H. J. Breuer, 56, 58, 118; C. C. Cooper, 37, 47; H. G. Cushing, 66, 68; Charles H. Davis, 67; Ruger Donoho, 46; Paul Dougherty, 67; J. J. Enneking, 71; Daniel Gerber, 68; Lillian W. Hale, 40, 65, 80; W. D. Hamilton, 55, 118, 120; Harry L. Hoffman, 118; James B. Hopkins, 45, 47; John C. Johansen. 68; Sergeant Kendall, 50; William L. Lathrop, 37, 50; Ernest Lawson, 73; Hayley Lever, 66, 67, 71; F. L. Mora, 45, 71, 117; Waldo Murray, 120; Elizabeth Nourse, 56; Joseph T. Pearson, 69; Marion Powers, 56; Ellen Emmet Rand, 65; Robert Reid, 45; William Ritschel, 68, 71; Edward F. Rook, 45, 48; Robert Spencer, 67, 68; H. O. Tanner, 117; Louis C. Tiffany, 71; Giovanni Troccoli, 48; Douglas Volk, 85; Robert Vonnoh, 45, 66, 70; Horatio Walker, 85; E. K. K. Wetherell, 70, 72; Irving H. Wiles, 70; C. H. Woodbury, 37, 69, 119, 120; Charles M. Young, 45.

Water Colors, Miniature Painting and Drawing

Medals of Honor. - Lillian Westcott Hale, 40; Laura Coombs Hills, 40, 118; Henry Muhrmann, 54, 72, 119, 120; Frank Mura, 54, 119; P. Walter Taylor, 26; Charles H. Woodbury, 37.

Gold Medals. - William Jacob Baer, 40; Jules Guerin, 40; George Hallowell, 40; Charles E. Hell, 36; Arthur I. Keller, 119; Henry McCarter, 26, 37; F. Luis Mora, 45, 117; Alice Schille, 37; Henry B. Snell, 69. 117, 119; N. C. Wyeth, 26.

Etching and Engravings

Grand Prize. - Henry Wolf, 30.

Medals of Honor. - D. A. Wehrschmidt, 119; C. Harry White, not hung.

Gold Medals. - Gustav Baumann, 34; Allen Lewis, 34; D. Shaw MacLaughlin, not hung; 3. Andre Smith, 32; Cadwallader Washburn, 32; Herman A. Webster, 32.

Sculpture

Medals of Honor. - Herbert Adams, 68, Colonnade; Karl Bitter, 66, 68; D. C. French, 40, 68, Rotunda.

Gold Medals. - Cyrus E. Dallin, 30, 32, 35, 36, 37, 63, 66, 73, 83, Colonnade; James E. Fraser, 68, 119; A. Laessle, 51, 66, 67; Paul Manship, 92, 93; Attilio Plccirilli, 23, 42, 66, 73, 83, Colonnade; Bela Pratt, 61, 66, 89, Colonnade; A. Phimister Proctor, 72; Arthur Putnam, 67; F. G. R. Roth, 66.

Medals

Medals of Honor. - John Flanagan, 38, 39.

Gold Medals. - James E. Fraser, 38, 39; H. A. MacNeil, 38, 39.

Argentine Section. - In Room 112.

Oil Painting

Medals of Honor. - Antonio Alice.

Gold Medals. - Jorge Bermudez, Alejandro Bustillo, Ernesto de la Carcova, Fernando Fader, Jose Leon Pagano, Octavio Pinto, C. Bernaldo de Quires, Eduardo Sivori.

Sculpture

Medal of Honor. - Pedro Zonza Briano.

Gold Medals. - Alberto Lagos.

Australian Section. - In Australian Pavilion.

Etchings and Engravings

Gold Medal. - Mrs. J. C. A. Traill.

Chinese Section. -

Water Color Painting

Medal of Honor. - Kiang Ying-seng, 94.

Gold Medals. - Su Chen-lien, 94; Kao Ki-fong, 94; Miss Shin-Ying-Chin, 94.

Sculpture

Gold Medal. - Teh Chang, 94.

Cuban Section. - In Room 20.

Oil Painting

Medal of Honor. - Leopoldo Romanach.

Gold Medal. - Rodriguez Morey.

International Section. -

Oil Painting

Medals of Honor. - Axel Gallen, Annex; Eliseo Meifren, Annex; Franz von Stuck, 108; Heinrich von Zugel, 108.

Gold Medals. - John Quincy Adams, Annex; Curt Agthe, 108; Conde de Aguiar, Annex; Gonzales Bithao, Annex; Istvan Csok, Annex; Harold Knight, Annex; Laura Knight, Annex; Heinrich Knirr, Annex; Lajos Mark, Annex; Julius Olssen, Annex; Leo Putz, 108; George Sauter, Annex; C. W. Simpson, Annex; Harold Speed, Annex; H. Hughes Stanton, Annex; Carlos Vasquez, Annex; Janos Vaszary, Annex; Valentin de Zubiarre, Annex.

Etchings and Engravings

Medal of Honor. - Frank Brangwyn, Annex.

Gold Medals. - R. G. Goodman, Annex; Willy Pogany, Annex; Bela Uitz, Annex.

Medals

Gold Medal. - Ede Telcs, Annex.

Italian Section. -

Oil Painting

Grand Prize. - Ettore Tito, 21.

Medals of Honor. - Onorato Carlandi, 21; Camillo Innocenti, 21.

Gold Medals. - Leonardo Bazzaro, 21; Italo Brass, 25; Emma Ciardi, 25; Beppe Ciardi, 25; Guiseppe Ciardi, 25; Umberto Coromaldi, 21; Visconti Ferraguti, 22; Domenico Irolli, 24; Enrico Lionne, 24; Guiseppe Mentessi, 25; Plinio Nomellini, 24; Feruccio Scattola, 25.

Sculpture

Gold Medals. - Luigi Amigoni, 23; Renato Brozzi, 23; Arturo Dazzi, 22; Guiseppe Graziosi, 23; Antionetta Pagliani, 23.

Japanese Section. -

Water Color Painting

Medals of Honor. - Ranshu Dan, 1; Toho Hirose, 1; Shoyen Ikeda, 2; Keisui Ho, 1; Tomoto Kobori, 1.

Gold Medals. - Bunto Hayashi, 1; Taisei Minakami, 1; Yoshino Morimura, 2; Hachiro Nakagawa, 10; Hosui Okamoto, 1; Tesshu Okajima, 2; Kangei Takakura, 2.

Ben Macomber

Sculpture

Gold Medals. - Choun Yamazaki, 4; Yoshida Homei, 4

Metal Work

Grand Prize. - Chozaburo Yamada, 4.

Gold Medal. - Kazuo Miyachi, 4.

Lacquer

Medal of Honor. - Jitoku Akazuka, 4.

Gold Medals. - Kozen Kato, 4; Hikobei Nishimura, 4; Mesanori Ogaki, 4.

Pottery, Porcelain and Cloisonne

Grand Prize. - Kozan Miyakawa, 4.

Medals of Honor. - Sosuke Namikawa, 4; Yohei Seifu, 4.

Gold Medals. - Eizaemon Fukagawa, 4; Yoshitaro Hayakawa, 4; Hazan Itaya, 4; Tomotaro Kato, 4; Shibataro Kawado, 4; Sobei Kinkozan, 4; Meizan Yabu, 4.

Dyed Fabrics and Embroideries

Grand Prize. - Jinbei Kawashima, 4.

Medal of Honor. - Seizaburo Kajimoto, 4.

Gold Medals. - Chokurei Hamamura, 4; Yozo Nagara

and Riyoshi Hashio, 4; Goun Namikawa and Torakichi Narita, 4; Saiji Kobayashi, 4.

The Netherlands Section. -

Oil Painting

Grand Prize. - G. H. Breitner, 113.

Medal of Honor. - M. A. J. Bauer, 113.

Gold Medals. - David Bautz. 114; G. W. Dysselhof, 113; Arnold Marc. Gorter, 113; Johan Hendrik van Mastenbroek, 114; Albert Roelofs, 113; Hobbe Smith, 114; W. B. Tholen, 113.

Etchings and Engravings

Gold Medal. - T. H. Van Hoytema, 115.

Norwegian Section. - In the Annex.

Oil Painting

Medal of Honor. - Harald Sohlberg.

Gold Medal. - Halfdan Strom.

Etchings and Engravings

Medal of Honor. - Olaf Lange.

Gold Medal. - Edvard Munch.

Ben Macomber

Sculpture

Gold Medal. - Ingebrigt Vik.

Philippine Section. -

Oil Painting

Gold Medal. - Felix R. Hidalgo, 98.

Portuguese Section. -

Oil Painting

Grand Prize. - Jose Malhoa, 109, 110, 111.

Medal of Honor. - Jose Veloso Salgado, 109, 111.

Gold Medals. - Artur Alves Cardoso, 109, 110, 111; Ernesto Ferreira Condeixa, 109, 111; Joao Vaz, 109, 110, 111.

Swedish Section. -

Oil Painting

Grand Prize. - Bruno Liljefors, 100.

Medal of Honor. - Gustaf Fjaestad, 107.

Gold Medals. - Elsa Backlund-Celsing, 104; Wilhelm Behm, 103; Alfred Bergstrom, 103; Oscar Hullgren, 103; Gottfrid Kallstenius, 100, 104; Helmer Mas-Olle, 102; Hehner Osslund, 102; Emil Osterman, 106;

Wilhelm Smith, 100, 103, 106; Axel Torneman, 100, 104.

Water Color, Miniature Paintings and Drawings

Grand Prize. - Carl Larsson, 101.

Medal of Honor. - John Bauer, 104.

Gold Medal. - Oscar Bergman, 101.

Sculpture

Gold Medal. - Gottfried Larsson, 100.

Medals

Gold Medal. - Eric Lindberg, 99.

Uruguay Section. -

Oil Painting

Gold Medal. - Manuel Rose, 19.

[1] For plan of rooms and national sections in the Palace of Fine Arts, see map on page 8.

Ben Macomber

XIII.

The Exposition Illuminated

First attempt to light an exposition indirectly, from concealed sources - Notable success of Ryan's work - Transformation of the Tower of Jewels - Details of his method - Weirdness of the Court of Ages at night.

Beautiful as the Exposition is by day, it is at night that it becomes loveliest as a spectacle. Then it is a great glow of soft color, without shadow, but also without garishness. Never before has the attempt been made to light an exposition as this one is lighted. The highest standard before attained was a blaze of electric light secured by outlining the buildings with incandescent bulbs. That was the work of electricians. Here the illuminators are artists who have created a great picture of light and color.

There is no blaze or glare. Light floods the Exposition, but from concealed sources. All-pervasive, seemingly without source, the illumination is rather a quality of the Exposition atmosphere than an effect of lights. Nor is it a white light. It is softened and tinged with the warmest and mellowest of colors. So mellow, indeed, is the illumination that it would not even be brilliant but for the radiance of thousands of prisms hung about the great Tower of Jewels, the intense light of which swathes the lofty structure in a pure glow, at once bright and ethereal. (p. 135.)

Above the glow in which the palaces are bathed, a pageant of light and color marches across the sky, a splendid aurora borealis, its bannered troops now wheeling in ordered array, now breaking their formation in wild riot, until out of the fantastic show huge beams of light separate to pierce the heavens.

This unique system of illumination, devised by W. D'A. Ryan expressly for the Panama-Pacific Exposition depends upon floods of light from concealed sources. Around the walls of the palaces stand tall Venetian masts, topped with shields or banners. Concealed behind the heraldic emblems are powerful magnesite arc lamps. These spread their intense glow on the walls, but are hardly recognized as sources of light by the passer-by on the avenues. Batteries of searchlights and projectors mounted on the tops of buildings light the towers, the domes, and the statuary. Even the banners on the walls are held in the spotlights of small projectors constantly trained on them. That there may be no shadows, concealed incandescent bulbs light up every corner and angle of the towers, the arches, and the cloisters.

The ghostly radiance of the Tower of Jewels comes from huge searchlights aimed at it from a circle of hidden stations. The many-colored fan of enormous rays, the Scintillator, which stands against the sky behind the Exposition, is produced by a searchlight battery of thirty-six great projectors mounted on the breakwater of the Yacht Harbor. It is manned nightly by a company of marines, who manipulate the fan in precise drills.

Ben Macomber

Concealed lights shine through the waters of the fountains. In the Court of the Universe they are white, the colorless brilliance of the stars; in the Court of Seasons they are green, the color of nature; in the Court of the Ages they are red, with clouds of rosy steam rising around them. Writhing serpents spout leaping gas flames on the altars set around the pool of the Ages, and from other altars set by the entrances of the Court rise clouds of steam given the semblance of flame by concealed red lights. By the high altar on the Tower of Ages the same device is used to make the lights flame like huge torches.

The palaces themselves are not lighted at night, though they have the appearance of being illuminated. Behind each window and doorway are hung strings of lights backed by reflectors. A soft glow of light comes forth, giving animation to the palaces and strengthening the picture outside.

There are two ways to see the Exposition at night, both of which must be followed if one is to get the fullest appreciation of the magic beauty of the lighting. One is to wander about the palaces and courts in the midst of the soft flood of mysterious light, watching the play of the fountains, the barbaric flames of the Court of Ages, the green shimmer of the waters in the Court of Seasons, the banners fluttering in strong white light, the statuary in changing hues according to the color screens used before the projectors, the Aurora Borealis above the Scintillator battery.

The other is from a distance. I have seen the illuminated Exposition from the top of Mount Tamalpais, whence it was a wondrous spectacle. But best of all I like to watch it from the hill at the corner of Broadway and Divisadero streets. It is best to go there early, before the lights are turned on. Then you may see the wonderful rosy glow of the Tower of Jewels and the two Italian towers before the white light of the projectors is flashed on them. Red incandescents are hidden behind all the columns of the Tower of Jewels and concealed in each of the Italian towers, as well as in the open spaces in and around the dome of Festival Hall. These are always turned on first. The Tower of Jewels then glows with a soft mellow red, less brilliant, but warmer and more colorful than its incandescence later on. The rich light wells up from the Italian towers and Festival Hall, and spreads from all their openings to stain the walls around with deep rose.

Then the ray of a searchlight falls on the Bowman atop the Column of Progress, silhouetting that heroic figure in the night as though he floated at a great height above the earth. Beams from other searchlights cause the Nations of East and West to stand out with startling distinctness on their triumphal arches; the great bulls of the Court of Seasons glow against the night; the golden fires are lighted in the Court of Ages. The tall masts around the palaces softly illuminate the walls. First one side and then another of the Tower of Jewels is bathed in white light, until the Tower stands out in ghostly radiance. Two slender shafts of light shoot upward on either side of the globe atop the Tower and stand there, symbols of pure aspiration reaching to the heavens. Behind it all the huge and many-colored fan of the Scintillator opens in gorgeous color in the northern sky.

The illumination is at its best on a misty night. Then its spectacular effects become more spectacular. The

Ben Macomber

moisture in the air provides a screen to catch the colored lights and make them visible in their fullest beauty. The Exposition recognized this need of a background for the great beams of the Scintillator when it provided for the clouds of steam that are nightly sent floating upward through the shafts of colored light. Nothing brings out the wonder of the Court of Ages at night like mist or fog. On the first night that all the illumination was given a full rehearsal it was raining slightly. The incandescence of the great globe of the Earth, the leaping flames on the altars by the pool, the rosy clouds over the bowls by the entrances and from the torches on the high Altar of the Ages, became strange, mystic, almost uncanny.

Of the beautiful light that falls upon the Palace of Fine Arts (p. 137), I can do no better than to quote from Royal Cortissoz: "At night and illuminated, it might be a scene from Rome or from Egypt, a gigantic ruin of some masterpiece left by Emperor or Pharaoh. The lagoon is bordered by more of those heavenly hedges that I have described. There are trees and thickets to add to the bewilderment of the place, to make it veritably the silenzio verde of the poet. And with the ineffable tact which marks the lighting of the Fair, this serene spot is left almost, but not quite, to the dim loveliness of night. The glow that is given its full value elsewhere is here at its faintest. The pageant ends in a hush that is as much of the spirit as of the senses."

XIV.

Music at the Exposition

Early neglect of music by the Exposition management remedied by the appointment of George W. Stewart, of Boston, as manager - Engagements of Camille Saint-Saens and the Boston Symphony Orchestra the musical events of the summer - Original compositions by the French master - Sousa and his great band - Other notable bands - Lemare's organ concerts- Splendid choral performances by famous organizations - A half-million for music.

Music cannot be omitted from any scheme of mundane celebration. In an exposition of the character of this one, where all art has been given so high a place, this gift of the gods must assume an unusual importance. It is important here, not only as a means of entertainment, but as a means of cultural development, and as an intellectual factor in the evolution of the race. This Exposition justifies itself by its storehouses of knowledge. Its reason for existence is, the permanent advancement of the people of the world in all that art, science, and industry, can bring to its palaces for pleasurable study.

With the agreement that a great pipe organ was to be installed in Festival Hall, and that orchestras and bands

Ben Macomber

were to be engaged, the early speculative musical labors of the directorate ended. Casual indeed was the attention paid to music during all of the early part of the pre-Exposition period. Material interests - and there were millions of them - cried for consideration, while the still, small voice of music was drowned in the clangor of construction. Just as music is the last of the arts to receive recognition at our universities, so it was neglected here until so much time had elapsed that only the most fortunate of accidents could give song and symphony their proper places among the wonders that were ultimately to find a home in the Jewel City. Fortunately, accident for once proved kind; vigorous direction emerged fortuitously from apathy.

In the early building period, President C. C. Moore turned aside from his other cares long enough to appoint J. B. Levison Chief of the Music Department. A better choice could hardly have been made. For more than two decades Mr. Levison, an able amateur in music, and a business man of high standing, had been identified with all of San Francisco's larger efforts in its musical life. But Mr. Levison's grasp of the importance of such a post was more comprehensive than President Moore's, for he refused the position. Fortunately, however, he had his attention directed to George W. Stewart, of Boston, a former artist of the Boston Symphony Orchestra, a man technically equipped, who had made a great success of the music at the St. Louis Exposition. Stewart was engaged, and to him is due the credit for the remarkable record music has already made at the Panama-Pacific Exposition.

Aside from the construction of the $50,000 pipe organ, which, after the Exposition, will be placed permanently in the Civic Auditorium, the two most important musical items found on the schedule of Exposition enterprises are the engagements of Camille Saint-Saens and the Boston Symphony Orchestra. The former, who maintained that "Beethoven is the greatest, the only real, artist, because he upheld the idea of universal brotherhood," is perhaps better fitted than any living composer to write special music for the Exposition. This he has done, - writing two compositions in fact; and their presentation has been an outstanding feature. "Hail, California," was dedicated to the Exposition. Scored for an orchestra of eighty, a military band of sixty, a chorus of 300 voices, pipe organ and piano, its first presentation was an event. The Saint-Saens Symphony in C minor (No. 3) Opus 78, composed many years ago, has become a classic during the life-time of its creator. It was one of the wonders of the Boston Symphony programmes played in Festival Hall. Its yield of immediate pleasure and its reassurance for the works of Saint-Saens to be heard later, grew from the fact that it was scored for orchestra and pipe organ, and in this massive tonal web the genius of the composer to write in magnificent size was overwhelmingly evident, thus forecasting the splendors of "Hail, California."

The other work written by this visitor from Paris is in oratorio form and titled, appropriately, "The Promised Land." A huge choir of 400 voices, directed by Wallace Sabin and named in honor of the visitor, the "Saint-Saens Choir," rendered a good account of the ensemble sections of the choral composition, while the Exposition orchestra of 80 instrumentalists and the Exposition organ added effectiveness to the accompaniment. Sabin presided at the organ. In addition to these appearances, the composer conducted three

Ben Macomber

recitals during the latter part of June, when all of the compositions offered were his work.

The visit of Dr. Karl Muck with his Boston Symphony Orchestra has become a luminous memory. The trip is utterly new in the history of music anywhere, nothing like it ever before having been attempted. It is said that the transportation bills alone amounted to $15,000, and there were no stop-overs en route for concert performances to help in defraying this bulky first cost. It is proper to record here the financial success of the venture. While the season of twelve concerts was yet young, more than $40,000 had been taken in at the box office, and the estimated expenses of $60,000 were liquidated, with a margin of profit. This was enhanced by an extra concert, the thirteenth. Tickets for the season were sold in Chicago, New York, Boston, Seattle, Spokane, Tacoma, St. Louis, Portland, Maine, and Portland, Oregon, while San Francisco and the bay communities in general sent their thousands to the glorious recitals. The result will be seen in a stimulation of music in the West.

But the engagements of Saint-Saens and Dr. Muck with his orchestra do not sum up the important activities of the Exposition's music. There are other features which challenge even these in popular estimation.

John Philip Sousa has spent a long season at the Exposition. A blunder was somewhere made in dating the arrival of the March King and his splendid instrumentalists, who came while yet the Boston Symphonists were playing in Festival Hall. As a result the finest of bands was placed in competition with the finest of orchestras. But nothing disastrous happened.

Those who desired, to the number of fifteen thousand, heard Sousa at his opening concert in the Court of the Universe; those who desired heard Dr. Muck's instrumentalists, to the seating capacity of Festival Hall.

Featured concerts have been and are being given by massed bands composed of Sousa's, Cassasa's, Conway's and other military or concert organizations.

Briefly, and regardless of the importance of each item, here are some of the attractions which make this Exposition vocal and harmonious: Edwin Henry Lemare, of London, by general critical agreement declared the greatest living organist, is expected here early in September, when he will begin his series of one hundred organ recitals, to continue till the Exposition closes in December. A unique episode of the Exposition music must not be overlooked in the recital by Madame Schumann-Heink, whose graciousness found another expression in her concert given exclusively and gratuitously to the children. More than three thousand of the little folk were in Festival Hall when the grandest of singers sang for them alone. The visit already accomplished of Gabriel Pares and his famous Republican Guard band of Paris; the engagement already begun of the Ogden Tabernacle Choir of 300 voices; the Eisteddfod competitive concerts; the long stay of the Philippine Constabulary band under the leadership of Captain W. H. Loving; Emil Mollenhauer's big Boston band; the concerts of the United Swedish Singers; the Apollo Music Club's premised visit from Chicago - the organization is coming intact with all of its 250 vocalists and its distinguished composer-conductor, Harrison M. Wild; La Loie Fuller's spectacles, and the engagement of

Ben Macomber

forty noted organists to appear in Festival Hall in addition to Lemare and Clarence Eddy, are a few of the accomplished or promised attractions. To this list must be added the daily concerts given gratis at different periods by various bands other than those named - the official Exposition band of 45 players under the seasoned direction of Charles H. Cassasa; Thaviu's splendid band of 50; Conway's military and concert band of 50, and others yet to be had in the world of music will be spread for their delecta-concerts are booked. As proof of the worth of these, let the achievements of the recent past speak. We have heard the Alameda County 1915 Chorus of 250 voices under Alexander Stewart in a majestic performance of Handel's "Messiah;" the Exposition Chorus under Wallace Sabin in a repetition of the music sung as part of the opening day's celebration - "The Heavens are Telling," from Haydn's "Creation," and the official hymn - "A Noble Work" - by Mrs. H. H. A. Beach; the Berkeley Oratorio Society under the inspiring direction of Paul Steindorff in two splendid concerts, the first given to Rossini's "Stabat Mater" and the second to Brahms' "German Requiem;" and the Pacific Choral Society's performance of Haydn's "Creation" under the musicianly leadership of Warren B. Allen. More music may confidently be looked for from these rich sources.

The Exposition authorities declare that half a million dollars will have been expended on music before the end of the life of the great enterprise. Thus visitors to the Exposition may come at any period of the Jewel City's existence, knowing that the best to be had in the world of music will be spread for their delectation, and that they will be afforded a comprehensive view of the art of tone as it exists today. In this respect the Exposition's musical "exhibit" is similar in its scope to the revealments in all its other departments; for the Exposition is avowedly devoted to contemporaneous rather than historic achievements.

Nothing that extends contemplation over a wider period than the last five years is admitted for competitive exhibition. The modern composer, no less than the modern inventor, is having his day at the Exposition. This is as it should be. We are hearing, have heard, or will hear, the last utterances of present-day musical creators. Indeed, in the case of one - Saint-Saens - we heard, as I have recounted, two massive compositions written expressly for the Panama-Pacific International Exposition, and John Philip Sousa has bent his most martial mood to the composition of an inspiring march which is called "Panama." But music also enjoys a privilege not accorded equally to any other department of Exposition display. The works of the past, as well as the present, are given. A history of music at the Exposition properly written - as one surely should be - would be an epitome of the evolution of the art from Cherubini, Haydn and Bach to Richard Strauss, Saint-Saens and Debussy. It would involve in its telling the stories of music in Italy, Germany, Austria, England, France, Russia, Scandinavia, yes, and America, too! It would include an account of the genealogy of the modern orchestra as exemplified in the Boston Symphony or the Official Symphony, and of military bands up to the perfected concert organizations headed by a Sousa or a Gabriel Pares. It would embrace with like inclusiveness the history of the pipe organ through its stages of evolution from the ponderous instruments with men straddling unwieldy bellows to the marvel installed in Festival Hall, and it would embrace the history of the art of organ music up to such exemplars as our own Clarence Eddy, John &.

McClellan, Edwin Lemare, and Camille Saint-Saens. What a chapter would be set aside for the record of Exposition choral music! Already there has gone abroad from the Festival Hall an impetus towards better chorus music that will, I feel sure, firmly establish this somewhat neglected department of musical art in the far West.

XV.

Inside the Exhibit Palaces

All competitive exhibits strictly contemporaneous, showing the arts of to-day - Revolution worked by the motion-picture theater in exhibition methods - The lessons of Machinery Palace - Coal and steam fast yielding to liquid fuels and waterpower and electricity - Life-saving devices, accident prevention and employees' welfare made prominent in Palaces of Machinery and Mines - A contrast in locomotives - Building a motor car every ten minutes - Co-operative exhibits in Food-Products Palace - Many great displays by the United States Government - Educational exhibits not duplicated, each state or city showing its specialty.

In its industrial displays, as well as its art, the Exposition keeps steadily in view the fact that it commemorates a contemporary event; it is contemporaneous, not historical. Hence it was decreed from the first that the exhibits must be the products of the last decade, a rule strictly observed save in rare cases where older forms have been admitted for comparison. The result is two-fold. The exhibits are condensed to the essential, giving room for a greater number of exhibitors; and the progress of the world is shown as of today.

Ben Macomber

Eleven palaces house the exhibits, exclusive of live stock. Officially, the things shown in the state and foreign buildings are not "exhibits," but "displays," and are not eligible for award. In general, the names of the palaces indicate the classes of exhibits to be found in them. No sharp line, however, can be drawn between the Palaces of Manufactures and Varied Industries, or between Agriculture and Food Products. In other cases there is some overlapping of classes. One section of the Liberal Arts exhibit is in the Palace of Machinery.

A striking feature of almost all the palaces, and one that differentiates this Exposition from its great predecessors of a decade or more ago, is the common use of the moving-picture machine as the fastest and most vivid method of displaying human activities and scenery. Everywhere it is showing industrial processes. Former expositions, for want of this device, have been mainly exhibitions of products. These have hitherto been shown in such bulk as to fill vast floor spaces and become a weariness to the flesh, while it was impossible, from the nature of things, to exhibit the great primary industries of field, forest, sea and mine in actual operation. The motion-picture machine has not only lessened the areas of products shown, thus making this Exposition more compact than former ones; but it has increased the effectiveness of exhibition methods by carrying the spectator, figuratively, into the midst of operations, and showing him men at work in all the important processes of agriculture, in the logging camps, in mines and fisheries, as well as in the mills and factories where the raw materials of these basic industries are worked into finished products. Its value for showing scenery, too, is fully utilized here. Many of the states and foreign countries employ it. Even faraway Siam uses it to instruct the Occident concerning her resources and people. Counting those in the state and foreign buildings, seventy-seven free moving-picture halls are to be found within the Exposition. Their efficiency is indicated by the crowds that throng them daily.

The Palace of Machinery holds three lessons for the observer. It shows not only the state of man's invention at the present moment, the increasing displacement of coal by hydroelectric plants and liquid fuels, but what is perhaps more significant, the changing direction of invention toward devices for human betterment. The Diesel oil engine and multitudes of electrical machines stand for the latest word in mechanical invention. The Diesel again, with a host of other internal combustion engines, the electric motors and waterpower plants, and the absence of steam machines, bear witness to the downfall of steam. But the great space given to safety devices, to labor-saving machines, to road-making machinery, and to mechanical devices for increasing the comfort of country life, are evidence of the part machinery is coming to play in the task of making life more livable. As an exhibition of modern mechanical invention, Machinery Hall is unique, as all this Exposition is unique. There is almost nothing in it that is not the product of the last ten years; it actually represents construction of the last two years. Indeed, the wholly contemporary nature of the exhibits leaves the visitor without visible means of comparison.

As at the Centennial Exhibition in 1876, a prime mover is the central figure in the building. There it was the immense Corliss steam engine. Here it is a Diesel, started by President Wilson by wireless on the opening day, and generating all the direct current used in the palace. Another commanding exhibit is a 20,000

Ben Macomber

horsepower hydro-electric generator, significant of the modern use of water-power. The United States Government is the largest exhibitor in the building, with numerous fine models of warships, docks, dams and submarine mines; torpedoes, artillery, armorplate and shells, army equipment, ammunition-making machinery in operation, light-houses and aids to navigation, and a splendid set of models illustrating road-making methods. Crowded out of its proper place in the Palace of Liberal Arts, the exhibit of the printing trades occupies a section here, including a huge color press turning out illustrated Sunday supplements.

The Palace of Mines and Metallurgy offers ample evidence of the great figure which steel now makes in the world, and of the vast extent of the petroleum industry. Here, too, as in Machinery Hall, accident prevention is emphasized. From this point of view insurance exhibits are not out of place here. The United States Steel Corporation, with its subsidiary companies, shows in this palace the largest single exhibit seen in the Exposition, save those of the United States Government. Noteworthy are its excellent models of iron and coal-mining plants, coke ovens. furnaces, rolling mills, docks, ships, and barges, and an extensive section devoted to the welfare of employees, with model playgrounds.

Many states and nations, and many world-famous mining companies are represented by exhibits of ores and metals, of mine models, and mining and metallurgical processes in operation. California shows a gold dredger and a hydraulic mine in operation. The great copper mines of California, Montana, Utah, and Japan, have installed significant exhibits. The United States Government operates in this palace a model mint, a model post office, and features a daily "mine explosion," with a demonstration of rescue work.

The Palace of Transportation places its emphasis on automobiles and roads, electric locomotives and cars, and the mammoth types of modern steam locomotives. All of these exhibits represent construction of the last year, with one exception. The first Central Pacific locomotive stands beside a Mallet Articulated engine, - an enormous contrast. One third of the floor space is filled with steam and electric locomotives and modern cars. Some are sectioned, and operated by electric motors, vividly illustrating the latest mechanical devices. Another third of the palace is devoted to motor cars. The Ford Motor Car Company maintains a factory exhibit in which a continuous stream of Fords is assembled and driven away, one every ten minutes.

Plans for a great exhibit of aeroplanes were destroyed by the war. The Exposition, however, maintains a constant exhibit of the spectacular side of aeronautics in remarkable flights by famous aviators. After Lincoln Beachey was killed in one of these performances, his place was taken by Arthur Smith, who was instantly crowned as a far more dazzling birdman. Two aeroplanes are the only representation in the palace. Steamship companies have erected here sections of their vessels. Railroads make interesting exhibits of scenery along their routes, of safety devices and of railroad accessories. The Canadian Pacific, Grand Trunk Pacific, Great Northern, Southern Pacific, Union Pacific, and Santa Fe systems maintain buildings of their own, exhibiting the scenery, agriculture and other resources of the country through which they pass.

Ben Macomber

The Palace of Varied Industries illustrates the enormous complexity of modern material needs. Packed with severely selected manufactures, it is made especially interesting by the many processes shown in operation. Cotton and woolen mills, linen looms, knitting machines, machines for weaving fire hose, a shoe-making factory, a broom factory, and many others, are particularly attractive because they are engaged in making familiar articles. The machines in use demonstrate the refinements of present-day manufacturing processes. The factories of many nations are represented in this palace. Germany makes here her largest exhibit, notably of cutlery and pottery.

The Palace of Manufactures differs from the Palace of Varied Industries as a bolt of silk differs from a bale of leather. Yet this general distinction between the finer and the coarser classes of factory products is not rigidly adhered to. The Palace of Manufactures is distinguished by a remarkable exhibit of fine wares by the Japanese, and another of commercial art from Italy. Fortunately this Japanese display is of goods in the ancient style, infinitely more interesting, though less significant, than the extensive exhibits in other palaces of Japanese wares manufactured in competition with Western nations. Most beautiful are the ceramics, the lacquered ware, and the silks. Great Britain is an extensive exhibitor of cutlery, pottery, and textiles. Manufacturing processes are shown in operation in this palace, though less than in the Palace of Varied Industries.

The Palace of Liberal Arts found its six acres of floor space insufficient. The exhibits, forming a remarkable demonstration of the breadth of applied science, embrace electrical means of communication, including wireless telegraphy and telephony, musical instruments, chemistry, photography, instruments of precision and of surgery, theatrical appliances, engineering, architecture, map-making, typography, printing, book-binding, paper manufacture, scientific apparatus, typewriters, coins and medals, and innumerable other articles. A great space is occupied by talking machines "demonstrated" in musical theatres, and by cameras. The American Telegraph and Telephone Company maintains transcontinental telephone connection between its theatre and New York, and gives daily demonstrations. The United States Government has installed a great variety of displays. Most striking, perhaps, is the section from the National Museum, where the most modern methods of exhibition are exemplified in cases containing human groups that are almost real life. The great pipe organ in Festival Hall is classed as one of the exhibits of this palace. Germany, Japan, China, the Netherlands, Uruguay, Cuba, and New Zealand are heavy exhibitors here. Of special interest is the German exhibit of radium and its allied metals.

The Palace of Education and Social Economy contains the special educational exhibits of this Exposition, which itself, as a whole, is a world-university. Its striking features are the great number of official exhibits by states, cities and foreign nations, and the emphasis laid on industrial and vocational education, public health, playgrounds, and the training of abnormal children. An educational exhibit is one of the most difficult to make vivid and interesting to the general public. This palace has succeeded by avoiding duplication. To each state or city was assigned a special problem, as far as possible the one to which it had contributed a noteworthy solution. Thus,

Ben Macomber

Massachusetts shows her vocational methods, while Oregon specializes on rural schools as neighborhood centers. Among the cities, St. Louis devotes most of its space to the educational museum, while Philadelphia emphasizes central high schools. The United States Government supplies a branch of its Children's Bureau, with daily conferences for parents. Among the many instructors who have been engaged to conduct classes in the palace is Dr. Maria Montessori, who is to give a course of lessons based on her famous system. The Philippine exhibit shows that Americans have developed in the Islands a system of practical education which American teachers should study.

The Palace of Agriculture is an instructive presentation of modern farm methods, as well as of raw products of the soil. It shows admirably the great advance in agriculture in the United States, giving due space to the work and influence of the state agricultural colleges. Particularly impressive is the array of farm machinery and the wide application to it of the gasoline motor. After seeing it, one wonders what place is left on the farm for the horse. The fundamental nature of agriculture has brought more states and foreign countries into this palace than are represented in any other. A significant representation is that of the Philippines, an exhibition of enormous natural resources. Its display of fine hardwoods is the finest ever made by any country. Similar exhibits of Argentina and New Zealand are also excellent. Forestry takes a large place in this palace, the United States Government making a big forestry exhibit in addition to the great general display of the Department of Agriculture.

The Palace of Food Products is a temple of the tin can

and the food package. It is made one of the most interesting of all the Exposition buildings by its numerous processes in operation. A large part of it is really a factory, turning out before the visitor's eyes the different familiar edibles of the magazine advertisements. A mint of money must have been spent by these exhibitors. A flour company, for example, has installed a complete mill in which flour is manufactured, and then made into many kinds of cakes and pastries by a row of cooks of various nations. A bakery in connection with this mill turns out 400 loaves at a baking. As in every exposition, visitors crowd the booths where edible samples are distributed. After viewing many such scenes, a local humorist dubbed this building "the Palace of Nibbling Arts."

The new idea of co-operation among manufacturers appears in a number of collective exhibits. California wine producers have united in a splendid display, far more impressive than could be made by an individual. The Pacific Coast fisheries have joined in an elaborate exhibit of every sort of tinned fish. The United States Bureau of Fisheries maintains an extensive aquarium of fresh and salt-water fishes. The State of Washington has another, with a salmon hatchery in operation. Modern production of pure food is greatly emphasized. In a building of its own, a Pacific Coast condensed milk concern operates a good-sized factory, using the milk of its herd of pure-bred Holsteins, kept in the Live-Stock section.

The Palace of Horticulture, with its gardens, has been planned with a three-fold purpose, to appeal with equal interest to the tourist, the student, and the business man. Its exhibits by states and foreign nations picture the gardens and orchards of the world. Its factory

Ben Macomber

installations exhibit actual processes of preparing and preserving fruit and vegetable products. Under the great dome are the Cuban and Hawaiian collections of tropical plants and flowers, already described in the chapter on the South Gardens. In the flanking rooms are displays of orchids and aquatic plants. In the main hall Luther Burbank shows his creations. An exhibit of fresh fruits in season is maintained. The gardens outside show plants and shrubs from many states and countries, including the great exhibit of the Netherlands Board of Horticulture.

XVI.

The Foreign Pavilions

Buildings characteristic of the nations represented - Many adaptations of famous old-world structures - Younger countries build expressions of their progress - Noteworthy pavilions of France, Holland, and the Scandinavian kingdoms - Italy's masterpiece in historic architecture - Argentina, Bolivia and other Latin-American republics well represented - Canada and Australia present fine buildings and splendid exhibits - China and Japan reproduce renowned gardens, temples and palaces - Rich treasures of art and industry shown by many countries.

Almost all the twenty-one foreign pavilions at the Exposition are characteristic of the architecture of the nations that built them. Some, like the unique Japanese temple or the beautiful French pavilion, are reproductions of famous old-world buildings. The three fine Scandinavian pavilions reflect notable types of national architecture. Italy's delightful group, which is the most noteworthy of all, is for every one who has visited that country an epitome of her most interesting historic palaces, rich in the art of the Renaissance. The buildings of the newer countries, like Canada or the Argentine, which have not yet had time to develop characteristic styles of their own , are admirable

Ben Macomber

expressions of their progress and prosperity.

Argentina. - The Argentine Pavilion is really a palace. It is the work of Sauze, a celebrated architect of Buenos Aires, in the style of the French Renaissance. (See p. 169.) The Argentino exhibits, with the exception of dioramas, moving pictures, and photographs, are in the Exposition palaces. The pavilion is the center for the social functions of the Commission.

Both exterior and interior of the building illustrate the amazing progress of the South American republic in art, as its exhibits in the Exposition palaces exemplify its advancement in industry and commerce. The entrance opens into a noble hall, imposing in its simplicity. In the clerestory the walls are decorated with fine murals by the brush of the Argentine artist, Colivadeno, - works which show that Argentine art has the beauty, freshness and vigor of the nation from which it springs. In the center of the hall is an exquisite bit of Sculpture.

On left and right the foyer opens into a fine reception hall and a graceful refreshment room. In the rear is a theater, where moving pictures of Argentine scenes are shown daily. In the wall of the corridor surrounding the theater on the first floor are excellent panoramas showing scenery and resources. Among these is a view of the famed Iguazu Falls, the greatest and most magnificent waterfall on the globe. In the corridor upstairs are other panoramas, a series of photographs, and a collection of graphic charts which show the commerce, finance, industry, administration, education and social service of the republic. The second floor ends at the rear in a beautiful library.

The pavilion was built entirely of materials brought from Buenos Aires, and constructed by Argentino workmen.

Australia. - The Australian Pavilion, at the Presidio entrance to the Exposition, was designed by George J. Oakeshott, F. I. A. N. S. W. (p. 148.) Obviously it is intended to symbolize the industrial cohesion of the six Australian States, New South Wales, Victoria, Queensland, South Australia, West Australia, and Tasmania. The facade bears below the cornice the titles of the states, with the state banner waving from a staff above. All are subordinated to the central tower, floating the flag of the Commonwealth.

Because its exhibits are eloquent of the resources of the great young country, the Pavilion has been described aptly as "the shop window of the Commonwealth." The building is, in fact, a huge sample room; and although the large states only, New South Wales, Victoria and Queensland, provided the display, each section is adequately representative of all Australia produces. Tropical fruits and other products from the northeast combine with the horticultural and agricultural products of the temperate zone. Minerals from the rich fields of all the states are grouped. The opals and gems from White Cliffs and Lightning Ridge in New South Wales vie with other precious stones from Queensland in forming one of the great attractions. Handsome building stones, including exceptional marble, are side by side with samples of the world-famous hardwoods and the scarcely known but beautiful cabinet woods from the Australian forest, while the pastoral areas have provided wonderful collections of wool, leathers, meat and by-products. The agricultural exhibits have attracted much attention,

Ben Macomber

and were so arranged as to show the productiveness of irrigated areas as well as of the country generally. Carefully prepared literature, distributed liberally, has been a feature of the efforts of the Australians. The commissioners have made it their boast that nothing has been exaggerated; everything is "real." Even art critics who visit the pavilion will not be disappointed, for on the walls they will find many paintings of merit by Australian artists, including loan collections from the National Gallery of New South Wales and the Victorian Art Society.

The Australian exhibits, unlike those of most other countries, have been grouped in this building, instead of being shown in the various Exposition palaces.

Bolivia. - Bolivia has erected one of the most essentially national pavilions at the Exposition, an admirable building that expresses equally the two elements of its population, the Spanish and the Indian. The building is Spanish in its solid rectangular plan; its entrance is copied from the portal of the Church of San Lorenzo, and its central patio fashioned after that of the old mint at Potosi. It is Indian in the curious carved work of the facade and the monoliths flanking the entrance, both being exact copies of ceremonial temple stones from the lake region of Bolivia. The building was designed by Dr. Calderon of the Bolivian Commission and Albert Farr of San Francisco.

Tropical plants and fruits are shown in the brick-paved patio. The rooms in the interior include a moving-picture theater, an art gallery and museum, with pictures by Bolivian artists, and relics of the civilization of the Incas. The national exhibits are shown in the Exposition palaces.

Canada. - The Canadian Pavilion is the largest of the foreign buildings, and the best example at the Exposition of businesslike advertising by a government. (p. 148.) Planned by a permanent commission which has had fifteen years of exposition experience, the Canadian exhibit, down to the last detail, is designed to advertise the country. Even the site, at the junction of the highways leading to the Live-Stock Section, was chosen to get the largest number of the kind of visitors Canada is most anxious to greet. The architects were Humphreys, Limited, of London.

Architecturally, the building is mixed classic, finished in the Exposition travertine. The maple leaf of Canada appears in medallions on the walls, the royal arms of Britain over the entrances, and the British lion on either side of the approaches. Canada's entire exhibit is here. Her commission cares nothing for awards, but is concerned solely with attracting settlers and capital.

With this in view, the chief feature of the display consists of Canadian landscapes, illustrating the agricultural, lumbering, mining, and shipping interests of British North America. The scenes are set to produce a remarkable perspective. The beholder seems to stand on rising ground, looking away over miles of country. In each view the foreground is enlivened with real water and either living or moving things. There is a panorama of the great wheat fields bordering on Lake Superior. Trains move from grain elevators in the interior to the docks on the lake, where model steamers ply on real water. Electricity supplies the power.

The largest scene of all is of Canada as it was and as it is. The foreground represents the North, when the Indian and the game had it to themselves. In the

Ben Macomber

background the visitor looks for miles down a broad Canadian valley filled with wheat fields and pleasant farms. Canada's wild life is represented in the foreground by splendid stuffed specimens, from the bear and the moose and the musk-ox to the marten and the muskrat, and from the great gray honker to the hummingbird. On the right, in a forest scene, is a beaver pond with dam and house, where the real beavers splash in the water. On the left of the scene, where a cascade tumbles into it, is a pool of Canadian trout, maintained in the wonted chill of their native waters by an ice-making plant under the scenery. Canada hopes to draw wealthy sportsmen and vacationists, who will then see for themselves the opportunities for investment. Some of her largest enterprises have begun thus.

The Canadian Pavilion makes no provision for social functions, but it is an attractive place, where everyone is welcomed. By common consent Canada has made the most effective exhibit of its kind at the Exposition.

Central America. - Guatemala, Honduras and Panama have each erected pavilions characteristic of Central American architecture. The Guatemalan Pavilion houses a display of the products of the forests, fields, and mines of the country, with coffee as its most notable exhibit. A native marimba band playing Guatemalan airs makes complete the Central American spirit of this pavilion. The Pavilion of Honduras, which might have been brought entire from Central America by a genie, contains a display of laces, woven hats, tropic ferns and flowers.

China. - The Imperial Audience Hall of the Forbidden City at Peking is reproduced in miniature in the three government buildings of the Chinese compound at the Exposition. The central pavilion is modeled after the great hall where for three centuries the Manchu emperors gave audiences. The two flanking structures, both alike, are copies of the buildings where court officials and the delegations awaited the coming of the Son of Heaven to the throne room. The pagoda and the tower at the left and right of the entrance are likewise copies of structures in the Forbidden City. All the buildings were constructed by native artisans, brought over from China for the purpose. The flag of the Republic floats from the tower, its colors from top to bottom standing in order for Manchuria, South China, Tibet, and Mongolia. The ancient dragon is absent, banished by the spirit of New China.

Within the three government pavilions are magnificent carvings, vases and lacquered furniture, old prints and paintings on silk. The priceless collection of the latter, shown here and in the Chinese section of the Fine Arts Palace, is the finest in the world, the property of a Chinese collector. Its pictures are a complete representation of Chinese painting for more than a thousand years. China is represented by exhibits in all the Exposition palaces, the most extensive participation by any foreign country.

Cuba. - The Cuban Pavilion, designed by Francisco Centurion, is a good example of Spanish-American architecture. It is distinguished by a square tower at one corner, a wide portico, roof of Spanish tile, and a central patio, designed for receptions. On the second floor is a great ballroom approached by a splendid stairway in the old Spanish style. Cuba's most striking exhibit at the Exposition is the display of tropical plants and flowers in the Palace of Horticulture.

Denmark. - Denmark, like the two other Scandinavian countries, has made her pavilion characteristic of her own national architecture. Though not in any sense a reproduction, the building finds its motive in Hamlet's Castle of Kronberg at Elsinore. The architect has softened the grimness and bulk of the ancient fortress into a pleasing building, that has the spirit of the gray land by the German Ocean, and the solid character of the Danes. The dim past appears in the great gravestones on the grounds, copies of monuments on ancient Danish barrows.

In the entrance is a tiled lobby, with the information bureau. Beyond is the "Garden Room," so styled because of its exquisite furnishings and abundance of cut flowers. To the left is a reception room, done in massive Danish decoration, with Danish woods and Danish furniture. A handsome cabinet of mahogany and hammered silver is its most striking piece. Other rooms also contain wonderful antique furniture. An assembly room with a raised dais, and mural decorations suggestive of Danish industry and commerce, is in the northeast corner. The building contains a number of paintings by Danish masters that are of great interest and value.

Funds for this pavilion were contributed by Danish residents of California. The Danish Government supplied the furnishings. No commercial displays are in the building.

France. - The Pavilion of France is a replica of the eighteenth-century home of the Prince de Salm, at Paris, now and for more than a century the Palace of the Legion of Honor. (p. 157.) The original building, in the soberer mode of the French Renaissance, was of

Caen stone, the effect of which has been reproduced in the present construction. The erection of this pavilion marks a record in work of such magnitude. On the outbreak of the war, all thought of participating in the Exposition was dropped; but later the American ambassador, Mr. Herrick, succeeded in persuading the French Government to reconsider its decision. The plans were cabled from Paris, at a cost of $10,000, and the structure was completed in sixty days.

More notable than the building itself, or its priceless contents, is the fact that these are here. That, in the midst of war and its demands, France should still find time for the ideal, and for this beautiful tribute to the long-standing friendship between the two countries, is a demonstration of French spirit and of French culture that will not escape the attention of any thoughtful American. For France herself, as it has well been said, her appearance here means as much as a victory on the battlefield.

The French Pavilion is a dignified and impressive structure, as those who recall the Legion of Honor Palace in Paris will understand. The entrance to the court is a triumphal arch flanked by double rows of Ionic columns on either side, with figures of Fame as spandrels. The arch is connected by lateral peristyles with the wings of the pavilion, the attics of which are adorned with has reliefs. Ionic colonnades extend along the sides of the court to the principal front of the building, which is decorated with six Corinthian columns, forming a portico for the main entrance. The portal opens on a stage, above which a great central hall, flanked by lesser halls, extends back through the palace.

Ben Macomber

But the glory of the building is in its exhibits. France poured out the treasures of the Louvre, the Luxembourg and the National Museum to adorn this pavilion. Fine as is the exhibit in the French section of the Palace of Fine Arts, the best pictures and Sculptures are shown here. In the Court of Honor stands the masterpiece of the master sculptor of modern times, "The Thinker," by Auguste Rodin. (p. 158.) In the galleries are his "John the Baptist" and other important bronzes. Vast, unique and of the greatest interest is Theodore Riviere's wonderful group in bronze representing a triumphant band of desert soldiers dragging captive the Moroccan pretender, secured in an iron cage. There, too, are splendid paintings by Monet, Meissonier, Detaille, de Neuvilie, and many other French artists approved by time. Magnificent old tapestries adorn the walls of the great hall, with modern hangings on the entrance stage. Two shrines hold relics of Lafayette and Rochambeau, sent by their descendants; and busts of Washington and Franklin stand on either side of the heroic figure of France at the entrance.

French manufacturers have sent here those commercial articles which French taste elevates almost to the standards of Art. Exquisite products of the jeweler, the perfumer, the milliner and the costumer, with fine fabrics that make France famous, are shown in the wings beside the Court of Honor. But the greater part of the French industrial exhibits are in the Exposition palaces.

Belgium also finds her place in the French pavilion, with an exhibit of great interest, including many admirable modern paintings, fine panoramas of Antwerp, Ghent and Bruges, and a collection of rare old laces that will delight the heart of every woman.

Greece. - The Greek Pavilion represents the latest addition of a foreign nation to the Exposition family. The building was begun by the Kali Syndikat, a German corporation, forced by the war to abandon its undertaking. In April, 1915, the Greek government bought the building and finished it in classic style. Its exhibits include two hundred and fifty replicas of the most famous of ancient Grecian Sculptures.

Italy. - Though other countries have built pavilions characteristic of their soil and people, or have lavished their money on splendid examples of exposition architecture, it has remained for Italy to present in a single group a summary of the best that art has produced in a national history of two thousand years. (p. 159.) The Italian Pavilion does not attempt to reproduce any one architectural masterpiece. It echoes many. Therein is the triumph of the architect. Without copying, Piacentini has suggested in this building much that is famous in the architecture of Florence, Venice, and Rome. It is itself a masterpiece.

The Italian Pavilion is an irregular group of seven structures, all connected by arcades except the last building to the east, a moving-picture hall. The main entrance is at the west, where a broad low flight of steps leads up to a plaza between two tall buildings irregularly placed. That on the right, in Fifteenth Century style, contains the offices of the Commission. The hall on the left, reminiscent of the Bargello, is devoted to a splendid collection of antique Roman, Grecian, and Italian art, shown by Signor Canessa. On either side of the entrance is a Roman "Discus Thrower" in bronze. The Bargello hall is connected by

Ben Macomber

an arcade with a square Etruscan tower, which in turn is similarly joined with other buildings that close the plaza on the east. In the rectangle between the two parallel buildings on the east, is a beautiful peristyled Venetian court, adorned with bronzes and marbles copied from originals in the Museum of Naples. In the center is a reproduction in stone and bronze of the well of the Palace of Campo San Giovanni e Paolo at Venice.

Of the two parallel buildings on either side of this court, the southern one is a Florentine structure containing a single hall devoted to purely governmental exhibits. The Tribuna between the two is the sanctuary of the pavilion, containing the portraits of King Victor Emmanuel and Queen Margherita, and portraits and relics of the great of Italy, explorers from Columbus to the Duke of the Abruzzi, scientists like Galileo, Galvani, Volta and Marconi, statesmen like Mazzini, and soldiers like Garibaldi. The other principal hall contains a series of rooms representing the cities of Italy during the Renaissance. First from the east is a reproduction of the Fifteenth Century library of the sacristy of the Church of Santa Maria alle Grazie at Milan, a chamber of beautiful armoires of carved wood, with panels painted with sacred pictures in colors. Next is a Neapolitan room, filled with reproductions in bronze and silver and marble of the Pompeiian treasures of the Museums of Naples and Rome. Then comes the Florentine Room, furnished in Fifteenth Century style with carved and inlaid wood, and adorned with copies of the best bronzes and marbles of the great mediaeval city. There is also a dining room in Fourteenth Century Florentine style, and then comes, at the western end, the Royal Salon, a magnificent hall with ceilings in blue and gold, and murals by Pieretto and Bruno Ferrari.

All the art works of the mediaeval rooms are copies of originals, but in the Bargello Hall, Signor Canessa, who was J. P. Morgan's European agent, shows his collection of veritable Italian and ancient art. Here are many things familiar through books, Michelangelo's bust of the Virgin; a cabinet full of reliquaries and profane vessels in crystal, gold and enamel done by Beuvenuto Cellini; the bronze Bacchante with silver eyes which was dug up in the gardens of the Persian embassy at Stamboul, and which dates from the Third Century B. C.; the famous portrait bust in rock-crystal of an Egyptian king of the Eighteenth Dynasty; madonnas and saints by Fifteenth Century painters; a complete garden set, fountain, statues and all, from a Pompeiian villa; Greek bronze and silver vessels and statuettes; Bernini's bust of the Cardinal de Medici; Fifteenth Century tapestries, and so many other objects of mediaeval and ancient art that a special catalogue has been prepared to describe them.

Italy's modern painting and Sculpture are well represented in the Palace of Fine Arts, and her industrial and commercial exhibits are in the other palaces.

Japan. - Japan has chosen her temple and palace gardens as the types to represent her at the Exposition. (p. 169.) She dug up the Mikado's private garden at the end of the sacred Red Bridge in Nikko, trees, shrine, rocks, greensward and soil, and set it down again on the Exposition grounds. So doing, she has shown the Western world a lesson in the beauty of simplicity. The central building in this charming garden is a copy, enlarged, of the Golden Pavilion of the Roku-on-ji

Temple in the city of Nara. It is of plain wood and lacquer, with interior walls and ceiling entirely covered with gold leaf. The office building joined to the temple was suggested by the shrine of the ancient castle of Fushimi. The exhibit building north of this temple houses a complete and remarkably beautiful fac-simile of the famous temple at Nikko, one of the finest in Japan. The Mikado's private collection of Japanese art, never before opened to the public, even in Japan, is placed in the Japanese section of the Fine Arts Palace. The paintings, scrolls, porcelain, satsuma ware, Sculptures and metal work shown in this very noteworthy exhibit were collected by the late Emperor Mutsuhito.

One of the tea houses is an exhibit of the Central Tea Traders' Association, the other one by the Formosan Government. The striking features of the gardens, beside the stream and the lakelet, are the dwarfed conifers, priceless trees. Two of them are the products of ten centuries of systematic pinching back. With them are three sago palms, five hundred years old. Scattered throughout the gardens are stone lanterns. Every plant, every bit of turf, every stone in the bed of the stream even, came from Nippon.

Japan is one of the largest exhibitors in the Exposition. Her displays, shown in every palace except Machinery, are an amazing demonstration of the degree to which she has entered the trade of the world.

The Netherlands. - In its domed pavilion, gay with many bannered staffs, the Netherlands has achieved one of the most striking buildings in the foreign section. (p. 157.) Its architecture is not representative of the traditional Dutch style but fulfills the modern ideas of the present-day school of builders in Holland. Most prominent is the clock tower, where a bell rings the hours.

Within, the pavilion presents Holland as one of the great colonial nations. Roughly, it has three divisions, devoted to the mother country, the Dutch East Indies, and the Dutch West Indies, in each of which industry and commerce is pictured in dioramas and exemplified by displays of products. Dutch girls in national costume serve visitors in the refreshment room.

Holland's most noteworthy exhibits are those made by the Board of Horticulture of the Netherlands in the gardens of the Palace of Horticulture, and her pictures in the Palace of Fine Arts. Holland sent to San Francisco ten carloads of rhododendrons, conifers, and bulbs. To install them she sent Mynheer Arie Van Vliet, the landscape engineer of the Peace Palace at The Hague. Her industrial exhibits are in the Exposition palaces.

New Zealand. - The New Zealand Pavilion is of mixed French and Italian styles. It was designed by Lewis P. Hobart of San Francisco, in collaboration with Commissioner Edmund Clifton. While it contains a representative display of the chief products of the youngest of the Dominions, the main exhibits are in the Palaces of Mines, Agriculture, and Food Products.

Norway. - Norway, like Sweden and Denmark, has succeeded admirably in reproducing its national spirit in its pavilion. The building is a long story-and-a-half structure, in the ancient Norse style, dominated by a beautiful tower on which is emblazoned the Norwegian coat-of-arms. The lower floor contains three large

Ben Macomber

dioramas of characteristic Norwegian scenery, and an exhibit hall wherein are shown products of the industries of Norway, especially her great maritime activities. As in the case of the other two Scandinavian countries, the sons of Norway in California built the pavilion, while the Norse Government provided the exhibits.

Portugal. - A sign of the glorious past, when Henry the Navigator made his country a great sea power with colonies around the globe, appears in the knotted cable that binds Portugal's Pavilion. The fantastic architecture of this little palace is also historically significant, for it was adapted from that of the Cathedral of Jeronymos, the Convents of Thomar and Batalha, and the Tower of Belem, built in celebration of Portugal's golden age of discovery. The style is known as the Manuelino. Antonio do Couto of Lisbon was the architect, assisted by the sculptor, Mota Sobrinho. The building has a local significance in California, where thousands of Portuguese have settled. In the pavilion is a display of laces, inlaid articles and wickerwork, exhibits which are repeated in greater variety and with other products in the Exposition palaces. The walls are beautified with a series of very remarkable photographs of famous Portuguese cathedrals.

Siam. - The Siamese Pavilion is a perfect example of the architecture of the Far East. It reproduces a pavilion on the palace grounds at Bangkok. It was first built there by native workmen, taken apart in sections and shipped to San Francisco to be set up on the Exposition grounds. Teak, sandal-wood and other rare Asiatic timbers are used in its construction. Hammered metal work, carved ivory, and tapestries form its interior decorations; but, in striking contrast to its ancient art and spirit, the building is a moving-picture palace where Siam's life and industry is shown.

Sweden. - Sweden has delighted everybody with her pavilion, a building finely representative of the people who built it, and with her industrial exhibit as well. (p. 160.) The pavilion combines the best in Swedish ecclesiastical and domestic architecture, the church tower and the gabled hall near the center, dwelling-house types at the ends. It was designed by Ferdinand Boberg, a noted leader in Swedish art.

The building is almost entirely filled with exhibits of Swedish industry, a presentation as good in its way as Canada's splendid picture of her great, hardly touched resources. The Swedish steel works have sent numerous models of locomotives, steamships, and machinery, and full-sized samples of smaller products. The government has furnished models of docks and bridges, of buildings and other engineering works. The familiar Swedish matches are here in pyramids. There are rooms furnished by Swedish artisans in birch and oak, with chandeliers of hammered iron, carpets from Swedish looms, and fine ceramics from the Swedish potteries. Other exhibits are in the Exposition palaces. In art, the Swedish collection in the Palace of Fine Arts is perhaps the most distinctive display made by a foreign nation.

Sweden's part in the Exposition was made possible by the Swedish citizens of California, who gave the funds for the pavilion, while the home government provided for the installation of the exhibits.

Turkey. - The Turkish Pavilion supplies the one touch

Ben Macomber

of Islam in the foreign section. The Ottoman building is a copy of the palace of Sultan Ahmed I at Stamboul, the summer home of the present Sultan. Within the pavilion is a ballroom, cafe, and lounging rooms. But the interest of the building, and of the little mosque behind it, as examples of Turkish architecture, is entirely overshadowed by the wonderful collection of rare rugs, beautiful brasses and carvings, and rich inlaid and jeweled ornaments, all part of the Sultan's treasures, and valued at $1,500,000.

XVII.

The State Buildings

A section full of historical and architectural interest - Many notable buildings simply furnish State headquarters, others contain important exhibits - California's great Mission structure - The remarkable display of her counties - New York's stately palace - Oregon's timbered Parthenon - Interesting chapters in American history told by the houses of Massachusetts, Virginia, Pennsylvania, Maryland and New Jersey - Fine buildings of the Western States - Attractive pavilions of the Philippines and Hawaii.

The state buildings at the Exposition fall naturally into three groups: those that reproduce or suggest historical structures, those characteristic in some way of their builders, and those that express the importance of their states by dignified architecture and significant exhibits. The richer the history of the state, the more likely its building is to reflect its past. Several states which possess famous historical buildings, such as Mount Vernon or Independence Hall, have either copied them or used their motives in the Exposition structures. Twenty-seven states, the Territory of Hawaii, and the Philippine Islands, are represented by twenty-eight buildings.

Ben Macomber

The California Building, Thomas H. Burditt of San Francisco, architect, by far the largest state building ever erected at any exposition, is an exceedingly happy treatment of the Mission style. (See p. 179.) Its commanding tower is better than anything ever done by the padres in California. From its facade, Fray Junipero Serra looks out over a charming garden, which, more than anything else, invests this building with the real spirit of California. It is a reproduction, even to the fountain, the pepper trees, and the old fashioned flowers, of the private garden of the Santa Barbara Mission, a spot where no woman treads. From this garden, enclosed by walls of clipped Monterey cypress, one looks at the tower and is at once translated to Southern California.

This building covers five acres, and is worthy to be ranked with the Exposition palaces. Under the tower is a fine vaulted loge and a reception room, both opening into a splendid balconied ballroom behind, all finished in the Exposition travertine. The walls of the reception room are hung with magnificent tapestries, loaned by Mrs. Phoebe A. Hearst. The west wing contains the administrative offices of the Exposition and the Woman's Board, and the directors' club rooms. The large eastern wing is entirely filled with the displays of the fifty-eight California counties. (p. 182.) These together form one of the most noteworthy exhibits in the entire Exposition. They demonstrate the fact that a multitude of other resources besides her gold entitle California to be called "the Golden State."

The Oregon Building, Foulkes and Hogue of Portland, architects, imitates, though it does not reproduce, the Parthenon of the Athenian Acropolis. (p. 191.) Doric marble is replaced by the natural columns of the great trees of Oregon, and the frieze of Phidias, by the fretwork of the bark of pine and fir. There are forty-eight of the great columns, the same number as in the outer colonnade of the Parthenon, and, coincidentally, one for each State of the Union. They were cut from among the largest of trees. The Douglas fir, next to the redwood and the sequoia the most massive of living things, furnished most of them. But the largest happen to be the two giant incense cedars, which stand on either side of the main entrance. These are eight feet and ten inches in diameter. Then there are two columns on the south side, both cut from a spruce that was four feet seven inches through at 101 feet above the ground.

In exterior proportions the building reproduces the Parthenon, but the Parthenon had a double row of columns around its porch, the Oregon temple has but a single row. In size it is considerably larger than the Partheon. The great flagpole is a single stick of Douglas fir, 251 feet long, set in a 200-ton block of concrete. The building contains an excellent exhibit of Oregon's resources.

The Washington Building, A. F. Heide of San Francisco, architect, is a striking example of the French Renaissance. (p. 191.) Unlike most of the state buildings, it is used largely for the exhibition of home products. Its motion pictures, its group of wild life, and its displays of agriculture, mining, forestry and fisheries, are all designed to advertise the remarkable scenery and resources of the Evergreen State. Washington is an important exhibitor in the Palaces of Horticulture, Agriculture, Food Products, Mines and Education.

The New York State Building is, next to that of

Ben Macomber

California, the largest structure erected by any state. (p. 170.) It is in every way a dignified and noteworthy example of the best modern civic architecture. Charles B. Meyers, of New York City, was the architect. The building is finished in plastic travertine. A magnificent entrance opens upon a wide central corridor. An assembly room, intended for the use of New York organizations, and a restaurant, pierce the second story. The other rooms on the first floor are devoted to the reception and convenience of New York visitors. On the other floors are the offices and apartments of the Commission, with a special suite for the Governor of the State. New York's official exhibits are in the several exhibit palaces.

The New York City Building, Bertram G. Goodhue, of New York, architect, is the only municipal building at the Exposition. It is a simple classic structure, housing an extensive display intended to demonstrate and promote municipal efficiency. Its exhibits, maps, models, photographs and charts, - admirably illustrate all sides of city government.

The Massachusetts Building, planned by Wells and Dana, of Boston, is a fac-simile reproduction of the Bulfinch front of the Massachusetts State House on a scale of two-thirds. (p. 181.) Within, as well as without, it is of commanding interest to every American. Its rooms are furnished with veritable colonial furniture. The club room to the right of the entrance hall is done in Jacobean style, the reception room opposite shows fine copies of Chippendale, Sheraton, Hepplewhite and Adams originals, and is hung with a long series of historic portraits, lent by Massachusetts families and the State Historical Society. On the second floor is a room filled with genuine old furniture by the most famous makers, fine colonial mirrors, and a Willard clock. The Governor's suite and the Commissioners' rooms are furnished with exquisite copies of colonial models.

The Pennsylvania Building, Henry Hornbostel, of Pittsburgh, architect. This interesting structure is reminiscent of Independence Hall, Philadelphia, though it is not a reproduction of the Cradle of Liberty. (p. 181.) Its plan was dictated by the necessity of a fireproof structure in which to house the Liberty Bell at the Exposition. Consequently, it is the solidest and most enduring of the state buildings. Besides the Bell, which is placed in the loggia, its most striking feature is the two fine mural paintings under the attic, from the brush of Edward Trumbull, of Pittsburgh, one representing Penn's Treaty with the Indians, and the other Pittsburgh Industries.

The New Jersey Building, Hugh Roberts, of Jersey City, architect, like those of Pennsylvania and Virginia, tells of the days of the Revolution. It is a copy of the old Trenton barracks, erected in 1758, and used alternately by British and Colonial troops during the Revolution. Within, its simple and comfortable appointments make it one of the most popular of the state buildings. A large lounge with blazing fireplaces, and furnished in white reed, occupies the entire central section. In the east wing are the offices and rooms of the Commission. The west wing contains the lobby and a reception room in which hang two large marines painted by N. Hagerup, of San Francisco. As the building is to be President Wilson's headquarters if he comes to the Exposition, a splendid suite, corresponding with the rooms occupied by General Washington, has been furnished and reserved for him.

Ben Macomber

The Maryland Building, designed by Thomas, Parker and Rice, of Baltimore, presents a fascinating study of colonial architecture in its reproduction of "Homewood," built by Charles Carroll of Carrollton in 1802. The present aspect of "Homewood" has been imitated in appearance of age given to the brickwork and the timbering. The contents of the building are no less delightful, historically, than the structure itself. The Colonial Dames of America have enriched the walls with original portraits of colonial celebrities, old prints, original grants by the Baltimores, and many historical documents and relics. Colonial furniture adorns the rooms. Few of the state buildings will so well repay a visit.

The Virginia Building, Charles K. Bryant, of Richmond, architect, is as significant historically as any on the grounds. It is a complete reproduction of George Washington's home at Mount Vernon, down to the spinning room, the detached kitchen and the servants' quarters, and furnished in part with Washington's own furniture loaned by Miss Nannie Randolph Heth, of Virginia, the official hostess of the building. There is Washington's chair, Mrs. Washington's work box, Nellie Custis' music stand, and many other relics of the Father of his Country. The remaining furniture, also loaned by Miss Heth, consists of antique specimens brought over from England in colonial days.

The West Virginia Building, designed by H. Rus Warne, of Charleston, W. Va., while not copying any individual structure, suggests well-known colonial types. Its veranda, in particular, is like that of the home of the Lees at Arlington. The chief room is the long reception hall, where logs always burn in a huge fireplace, typifying the warmth of West Virginian hospitality.

The Mississippi Building, Overstreet and Spencer, of Jackson, architects, was designed to suggest the old-style Southern mansions. Some of its motives, especially the pillared portico, were taken from the old capitol building at Jackson. The displays contained in it are chiefly agricultural. Mississippi is also represented in the Exposition palaces.

The Ohio Building, designed by Albert Pretzinger, of Dayton, is a copy, on a smaller scale, of the classic State House at Columbus. Containing no exhibits except the relics shown by the State Historical Society, the building serves the social side of Ohio's participation in the Exposition. Its upper floor is entirely occupied by suites for the Governor and the Commissioners.

The Indiana Building, designed by J. F. Johnson, of Indianapolis, represents a type of modern Hoosier dwellings. It is of permanent construction, of sandstone and brick with a tiled roof, and unique in the fact that all of the materials used and all the furnishings are Indiana products. State pride appears again in the library of 15,000 volumes, confined entirely to the works of Indiana authors and books about Indiana. In addition to the building, which is wholly an exhibit, Indiana is well represented in the Exposition palaces.

The Illinois Building, designed by State Architect James Di Belka, of Chicago, is perhaps the best exhibit of the State at the Exposition. (p. 180.) It is a dignified three-story structure of the Italian Renaissance. The Sculptured tablets of the facades represent the history and progress of Illinois. The exhibits within are of unusual interest. The Lincoln Memorial Room, made possible by Mrs. Jessie Palmer Weber, contains a great collection of photographs, letters and relics of Lincoln, and many articles connected with his life. The valuable series of films prepared by the Chicago City Planning Commission is shown in the moving-picture hall. This building contains a fine pipe organ on which frequent recitals are given.

The Wisconsin Building, designed by R. A. Messmer & Co., Milwaukee, in the colonial style with wide porticoes, contains one of the State's best exhibits in its interior finish of fine Wisconsin hardwoods. The floors are all of maple and the paneled wall of birch. "Old Abe," the famous Wisconsin war eagle, stands above the main entrance. Over the fireplace in the reception room is a panel in relief, "The Progress of Wisconsin." The building is used a headquarters for Wisconsin visitors.

The Iowa Building, Clinton P. Shockley, of Waterloo, IA., architect, is a classic structure, finished, like most of the state buildings, in the Exposition travertine. It does credit to the public spirit of Iowa business men, who, in default of a legislative appropriation, supplied the funds.

The Missouri Building, designed by H. H. Hohenchild, of St. Louis, is a structure of real distinction in the Georgian style. (p. 180.) It copies no Missouri building, and is historical only in its pleasant combination of architectural features much used in early days. The building is of permanent construction and after the Exposition closes is to be turned over to the Government as a club house for the army, - this as a compliment to Major-General Arthur Murray, who, like so many other eminent Americans, hails from Pike County. The Missouri Home, as it is called, is used as a gathering place for visiting Missourians, and for the strong Missouri Society of California.

The Kansas Building, Charles Chandler, of Topeka, architect, is a pavilion in the style of the Italian Renaissance. It is a club house, devoted solely to the comfort and entertainment of visitors. Strong exhibits are made by the state in the palaces of Agriculture, Horticulture, Food Products, Education, and in the Live-Stock Section.

The Arkansas-Oklahoma Building, designed by George R. Mann, of Little Rock, was built and furnished by private subscriptions by citizens of the two states. It is a roomy bungalow designed for the convenience of visitors from Arkansas and Oklahoma, and exhibits some of their products.

The Texas Building, Page and Brothers, Austin, architects, is a pleasing example of Mexican architecture as distinguished from the California Mission style. It suggests the Alamo, and bears the Lone Star pierced through its raised cornice. Within is a patio, reached by broad entrances from the verandas at front and rear. A motion-picture hall, a ballroom, offices and rest rooms occupy the greater part of the building. The state exhibits are in the Exposition palaces.

The North Dakota Building, Joseph B. De Remer, formerly of Grand Forks, now of Los Angeles, architect, owes its unique ground-plan to a three-cornered lot. That it is a pleasing structure is witnessed

Ben Macomber

by several dwelling houses now being built in California after its plans. The building is French in style, treated in a simple manner. It contains interesting exhibits of the products of the Northern State, including a noteworthy display of pottery made at the University of North Dakota, an institution which devotes much of its effort to promoting state industries.

The Montana Building, Carl Nuese, San Francisco, architect, is one of the group of classic structures finished in plastic travertine. The only display made in the building, which serves as a social center for visitors from Montana, is a school exhibit. The State is, however, largely represented in the Palaces of Mines, Agriculture and Horticulture.

The Idaho Building, Wayland and Fennell, of Boise, architects, was the first state structure completed at the Exposition. It is built in the manner of the Italian Renaissance and looks out over the bay. Like most buildings of the Western states, it is equipped with a moving-picture theatre, as well as rooms for visitors. Idaho's exhibits are chiefly in the Exposition palaces.

The Nevada Building, designed by F. J. De Longchamps, of Carson, is another structure in the style of the French Renaissance. It is the headquarters of the Nevada Society of California and of visitors from the Sagebrush State. Nevada has important exhibits in several palaces.

The Utah Building, Cannon and Fetzer, of Salt Lake, architects, is a classic structure with deep porticoed front. All its furniture is an exhibit, made by the pupils of the manual training department of the Utah schools. The building contains interesting models of copper and gold mines, and an exhibit of the processes of salt-making, displays of building-stone, grains and grasses, and collections from the cliff dwellings. Other exhibits are in the Palaces of Mines, Education and Horticulture.

The Hawaiian Building, C. W. Dickey, of Oakland, architect, excellently represents the Pacific isles. In style it is French Renaissance, built with a half rotunda at the rear to accommodate a semi-circular aquarium. In the center of the main hall is a clump of palms and tree ferns, and native singers give the island touch. The aquarium contains a wonderful collection of the many-hued fish of the South Seas. Interesting displays of native cabinet woods are made in the finish of the offices. Though small, the Hawaiian building has proved one of the most popular.

The Philippines Pavilion, designed by the Bureau of Architecture, is one of the Exposition places which no one should miss. It marks the creation of an original style of exposition building. It is Filipino in all its motives. Its groups of four columns suggest the four essential posts of native hut construction; the broad roofs are tiled; the windows are not glass, but of thin shell, the common material used in the islands; the walls are finished in split bamboo matting. The same style of construction is used also in all the Philippine booths in the palaces. The materials are used with restrained taste, and this, with the magnificent cabinet woods employed throughout the construction, has resulted in a beautiful building. It is a little hard to realize the richness of the woods used here. The very floors in the pavilion and the booths are good enough to make piano cases of. The central portion, upstairs and down, is floored, wainscoted and ceiled with the

Ben Macomber

costliest of timber. The two offices to right and left of the main entrance are finished in a beautiful, hard, heavy rosewood, called narra, the one to the right in yellow narra, that on the left in red narra. The stairway is of a magnificent, richly figured, claret-red hardwood called tindalo, the favorite material for such construction in the islands. The panels of its wainscoting and the balusters are of a dark velvety epil, so dark and so glossy in some places that it looks almost like agate. All the columns are natural trunks of the palma brava.

XVIII.

The Live-Stock Exhibit

The first Exposition to offer a live-stock exhibit covering its entire period - Prizes total $440,000 - Classification of competitions - New methods of displaying herds and flocks - Contests in dairy and beef cattle - Other exhibits range from high-bred horses, hens and sheep down to pet rabbits, rats and mice.

For the first time in the history of similar celebrations, this Exposition offers a continuous live-stock show. Other expositions have confined their live-stock exhibit to a few weeks during the time of award-making. Here, however, the show extends from the opening of the Exposition until its closing. The competitive period extends from September 23 to December 3. Naturally this will mark the high tide of the display. During this time the International Jury on Awards will distribute in cash prizes a total of $440,557. Of this amount, $190,000 has been given by the Exposition management, $100,327 by the breed record associations of the country, and $150,230 by various states to be used in prizes and the transportation of stock.

These attractive prizes will be distributed, among the

Ben Macomber

well-established and well-known breeds of draft and light horses, ponies, beef and dairy cattle, sheep, swine, poultry, pigeons, and pet animals. All animals will be judged according to the rules of recognized breed associations. Foreign or other animals not recorded in the books of the associations named in the premium list will be judged by the standards of the associations to which their exhibitors belong.

The educational value of the live-stock show for the general public, as well as the stock breeder, has been emphasized in every department. The increased cost of living being a dominating topic for both producer and consumer, much attention has been centered on meat-producing animals. Liberal provision has been made in the prize list for fat classes in beef-cattle, sheep and swine.

When the Exposition management designed the live-stock section and planned the buildings for the various features of this department, an effort was made to create a model arrangement for exhibit purposes. So successful was this effort that a number of states have requested the plans for a ground layout. This portion of the Exposition cost the management approximately $150,000, and covers sixty-five acres. The buildings represent, in their equipment, the very latest development in the housing and caring for stock. The visitor first approaches from the east a quadrangle of eight large stables, enclosing the forum where the live-stock shows are held. These stables have a total accommodation of 1124 horses. The forum has a seating capacity of 2680 persons.

To the north of the stable quadrangle is Congress Hall, for the accommodation of conventions and other meetings, and containing also the administration offices of the chief of the live-stock department. On this side also are the corrals, feed storage barns, a service yard, and an area for open-air exhibits. To the south is the large dairy building, a dairy manufactures building, and the poultry exhibit building. The dairy building houses more than 300 animals. West of the stable group is the mile racecourse with its polo and athletic field.

One of the novel features of this show is the manner in which the view herds and flocks are displayed. These are seen in stalls and pens built at an angle of about forty-five degrees to permit the visitor to get a side view of the stock. The view-herd idea in itself is something new. These exhibits are purely educational in purpose, and non-competitive. They have been on display since the opening, and will continue until the close of the Exposition, thus enabling the visitor to see a creditable live-stock show, no matter at what season he may come. The view herds are selected by competent authorities, and represent the best of their respective breeds. Among such herds on exhibit are Shorthorn cattle, Berkshire swine and Percheron horses. These exhibits are changed from time to time.

In addition to these general features, the special events include the milk show, harness races, universal polo, wool grading, sheepdog trials, poultry show, and an international egg-laying contest.

For eleven classes of dairy cattle the Exposition offers awards, as follows: Jersey, Ayrshire, Guernsey, Holstein-Friesian, Dutch-Belted, Dairy Shorthorn, Brown Swiss, French-Canadian, Simmenthal, Kerry and Dexter, and Grade-Dairy Herd. This last is a

Ben Macomber

recognition on the part of the Exposition of the great utility value of the grade-dairy cow, which forms the basis of the dairy industry, and yet could not exist without the pure-bred stock. In the beef-cattle group, the Exposition offers awards in the following classes: Short-Horn, Hereford, Aberdeen-Angus, Galloway, Polled Durham, Red Polled, Devon, Fat Cattle (by ages) and Car-lots.

One of the especially attractive features pertaining to the dairy section is the exhibit of 150 high-grade Holsteins for utility purposes. This herd is in full flow of milk and is maintained by a large milk condensing plant. This exhibit, in the daily care given these perfect specimens of dairy cattle, the yield of Milk, the quality of feed and the appliances used, forms one of the most attractive units in the department. An important event in this section was the pure milk and cream contest, June 14 to 19, in Congress Hall. City and state boards of health and the dairy divisions of agricultural colleges participated in the contest. The purpose of the event was designed to create a greater interest in pure milk and cream. Four samples of milk and cream each were submitted. One of these was submitted to an official bacteriologist, a second given to the official chemist, a third displayed in Congress Hall, and the fourth tested for its butter-fat content. Awards of gold and silver medals and cash prizes were made in the following classes: city boards of health, cream dealers, milk dealers, college experiment stations, pasteurized milk, pasteurized cream, market milk producers, certified and medical milk commissions.

In the horse exhibit the following classes are provided: Percheron, Belgian, Clydesdale, Shire, Suffolk-Punch, Standard Trotter, Thoroughbred, Saddle Horses,

Morgan, Hackney, Arabian, Shetland Pony, Welch Pony, Roadsters, Carriage Horses, Ponies in Harness, Draft Horses, Hunters, Jumpers, and Gaited Saddle Horses. Among special events in this section are the following: trot under saddle, one-mile track, one-mile military officer's race, one-mile mounted police race, gaited saddle race of one mile, steeple chase, hurdle race, polo pony dash, relay race of one mile, cowboy's relay race of same length, cowgirl's relay race, six furlongs, saddle tandem. Exposition jumping contest and five-mile Marathon four-in-hand. On the closing day of the Exposition there will be a grand parade of all first and second winners, not only in the horse display, but in all other displays in this department.

The following dates have been set for the exhibition of stallions and mares in the breeding classes in the Forum: Thursday, September 30, - Percheron, standard trotter, Welch pony, and Morgan; Friday, October 1, - Belgian, Thoroughbred, Hackney, and Shetland Pony; Saturday, October 2, - Clydesdale, Saddler, Arabian, and Suffolk-Punch; Monday, October 4, - Shire, Jacks and Jennets, and Mules.

The exhibition of horses for awards is from Thursday, September 30, to Wednesday, October 13. One of the important events of this period is the special horse show. Two other big special events are the races and international polo tournament. The polo tournament from March 7th to May 1st enlisted the following teams: Cooperstown, N. Y.; Philadelphia Country Club; Midwick Polo Club; Pasadena, Burlingame and San Mateo Clubs; Boise, Idaho, team; Portland, Oregon, team; First Cavalry, Monterey; Second Division Army, Texas City, Texas; and Southern Department Army, San Antonio, Texas.

Ben Macomber

The Exposition harness races cover two periods, one from June 5 to June 15, and the other from October 30 to November 13. In addition to these there will be matinee races from May 23 to September 30. A total of $227,000 has been set aside for purses in these races.

The poultry exhibit for award is scheduled from November 18 to 28. This is known as the Universal Poultry Show, and is planned to be one of the largest ever held. Between 10,000 and 12,000 chickens, entered from all parts of the Union, will be in competition. In conjunction, the American Poultry Association meets in Congress Hall in the live-stock section. The International Egg-Laying Contest, extending over a period of one year from November 15, 1914, has attracted widespread attention. Pens of fowls have been entered in this contest from the United States and Canada, and even distant England. Daily records are kept of the production of each hen, and, once a month, the score is bulletined by the live-stock department for the information of owners.

Sheep and goats are to be judged for awards from Wednesday, November 3, to Monday, November 15. The breeds classified are: Shropshire, Hampshire, Cotswold, Oxford, Dorset, Southdown, Lincoln, Cheviot, Leicester, Romney, Tunis, Rambouillet, Merino-Ameiran, Merino-Delaine, Corriedale, Exmoor, Persian Fat-Tailed, Karakule, and car-lots; goats, Toggenburg, Saanen, Guggisberger, and Anglo-Nubian breeds, with the grades of each breed, and native goats.

The exhibit of swine for awards runs between the same dates. The eligible breeds, besides swine in car-lots, are Poland-China, Berkshire, Duroc-Jersey, Chester

White, Hampshire, Tamworth, Mule Foot, Large Yorkshire, Large English Black, Victoria, Essex, and Cheshire.

The scope of the live-stock department is not limited to the material things of rural life. A Universal kennel show is scheduled from November 29 to December 1. Two classes of dogs are provided for in the awards, sporting and non-sporting. A cat show, of long and short-haired cats, is set for the same period as the kennel show. Other groups of exhibits in this line are pet stock, rabbits, hares, rats and mice, and children's pets.

XIX.

Sports and Games; Automobile Races; Aviation

Exposition contests include nearly every branch of sport - National Championships of the A. A. U. - Two great automobile races, the International Grand Prix and the Vanderbilt Cup, already run - Polo and Golf - Sensational flights of the aviators - The International Yachting Regatta and other aquatic events - All-star baseball expected in the fall.

An account of the Exposition, and indeed, American athletic history for the year 1915, would be incomplete without a description of the sports programme. This outline of games and exhibitions includes nearly every branch of sport familiar to the American public, and its wide appeal has attracted many thousands to the athletic fields and gymnasiums of the Exposition. Although ten months of sport was originally intended by the athletic committee, this period has been somewhat abbreviated by circumstances, though a practically continuous performance has held sway since February 22.

International competition, at first intended in many branches of the programme, was generally abandoned on account of the European conflict; but the want of foreign representation has in no way lessened the quality of competition, or dampened the attractiveness of the summer contests. Some of Europe's star track men are entered here, in spite of conditions on the continent.

Perhaps the most popular attractions of the programme are the national championships, held every year under the auspices of the Amateur Athletic Union. At the convention of that body during November, 1913, prior to the death of its president, James E. Sullivan, it was voted unanimously to award all of the organization's events, with the exception of boxing, to the Panama-Pacific Exposition. These championships are the blue-ribbon events of the amateur world. They include track and field games, swimming, boxing, wrestling and indoor gymnastics. Three of these championships were staged in San Francisco before the opening of June.

In basket ball, the first of the national competitions, premier honors went to a California organization, the San Francisco Olympic Club. Next in line came gymnastics, followed by wrestling. Although these sports are not immensely popular with the athletic enthusiasts, generous galleries turned out to see the American champions in action.

The more important part of the Amateur Athletic Union programme was scheduled for the summer months, when the track and field championships are held. Facilities for staging these games are ideal. The cinder path, situated at the far end of the Exposition grounds, with unexcelled scenic advantages, is reputed to be the equal of any athletic stadium in the country. The oval measures one-third of a mile to the lap, with a 220-yard straightaway flanking the grandstand. The earlier games convinced Eastern athletes that there could be no complaint against facilities.

The senior and junior track and field championships of the Amateur Athletic Union loom up as the banner track events of the programme. National stars have signified their intention of participating in these games, and it will be surprising if many national records are not broken. In addition to these games, the International Olympic Committee, which controls all the modern Olympic meets, conferred upon the Exposition the right to hold the Modern Pentathlon, this being the first time it has been contested outside of the Olympic Games. In addition, America is to have for the first time the Decathlon, and the famous Marathon race originated in Greece centuries ago, and impressively revived during recent years by the more important athletic bodies of the world.

Besides the Amateur Athletic Union track and field games, an abundance of competitions, ranging from grammar school contests to collegiate struggles, was arranged. Among the first of these, the Pacific Coast Intercollegiate Conference, was won by the University of California from a field of collegiate teams representing the entire Pacific Coast. Several high and grammar school contests have attracted spectators to the stadium. One thousand grammar school athletes entered the lists upon the Exposition cinder path, and staged a carnival that stands as a record in California, and approaches any American event of its kind both in the number of entrants and the class of competition offered.

Automobile racing, of the kind that thrills, was furnished by the Exposition during its early weeks. Two events of international importance were run upon the Exposition grounds, and in each instance attracted one hundred thousand spectators to the course. The first of these was the International Grand Prix, run in the rain and under other conditions far from ideal, over a four-mile course for the distance of four hundred miles. Sensation followed sensation in this feature, a final winner being supplied in the swarthy Darius Resta, who drove a Peugeot car for an average speed of fifty-six miles, 7:07:57 being his actual time. Other drivers of international reputation appeared in this struggle, among them De Palma, Hughes and Wilcox. Handsome prizes were distributed to the winners in these events.

The Vanderbilt Cup Race was staged over the same course on March 7, and brought out an equally attractive field. Running with the precision and dexterity that brought him home a winner in the Grand Prix, Resta repeated his victory in the Vanderbilt Race, coming home from his journey of three hundred miles ahead of such stars as Burman, Pullen, Wilcox and De Palma. Resta earned the reputation of being one of the most skillful drivers holding the wheel in this or any other country.

For six weeks, from March to May, polo held popular sway at the Exposition. Ten teams competed in a tournament which offered many valuable trophies. The contests were held daily and attracted thousands to a specially prepared turf field near the athletic stadium. The sport furnished thrilling competition throughout its period.

Perhaps the most famous team seen in competition was the noted four from Cooperstown, New York, bearing an international reputation. The Easterners, although

Ben Macomber

weakened by illness in the ranks of their players, proved practically invincible. Another notable organization was the four representing the Midwick Club of Pasadena, California. In addition to the civilian teams, the United States army was represented by some fast fours, who provided thrill after thrill with their reckless but winning form in the saddle. Perhaps the most notable of the military combinations was the Fort Sam Houston four, which went through the tournament with practically an undefeated record. The army teams were granted certain handicaps, however, which gave them a slight edge in some of the contests.

Aviation, a branch of sport which claims a large place in the popular fancy, was not neglected by those who drew up the programme. Two world-famed aviators have performed before hundreds of thousands, though one of these, Lincoln Beachey, became a victim to the elements which he had so often defied. While giving an exhibition flight in a German Taube, Beachey fell to his death on March 14 when his monoplane crumpled at the start of a daring loop.

Nothing daunted by the untimely end of Beachey, a new luminary appeared in Arthur Smith, whose aerial maneuvers exceed in point of recklessness anything attempted by his predecessor. Smith thrills thousands in daily flights and skiey acrobatics, including crazy dips and loops, startling dashes to the earth and illuminated flights through the night air. (See p. 192.) Smith became in a day an attraction outshining, perhaps, any other single performer upon the huge Exposition programme.

Those who loved horse racing and grieved at the decline of the sport in California, were rejoiced at the announcement of some of the biggest harness and running events yet staged in this country. Two meetings were arranged for the Exposition schedule, a summer harness event, June 5th to 19th, and a fall running meeting, October 30th to November 13th. The Panama-Pacific is the first Exposition to make horse racing an outstanding feature of its activities. About $227,000 was set aside to be distributed in handsome purses and stakes for the events. A $20,000 trotting and a $20,000 pacing stake was put up for each meeting, with other sums ranging from $1,000 to $5,000. The four stakes of $20,000 each are the largest ever offered in any light-harness event, and insured entries of the highest class.

The race track is situated near the athletic stadium, and commands an unsurpassed view of the San Francisco Bay, together with the Marin County heights and the entrance to the Golden Gate. The grandstand seats thirty-five thousand spectators. The course, under scientific preparation for several months, was put in fine shape. The length of the lap is one mile.

One of the biggest golf events ever staged in this country was successfully managed by the Exposition. Five weeks of sport on the links around the bay counties, including high-class exhibitions by both men and women, were in the plans of the committee. Events included both professional and amateur contests, and seldom, if ever before, had a community of the size of San Francisco maintained so continuous an interest in the sport. Valuable prizes and trophies were offered for the different events of the programme. Handsome cups and medals were granted amateurs, while professionals were tendered purses of generous proportions.

Ben Macomber

Perhaps the banner event of the tournament was the amateur championship for men played on the course of the Ingleside Golf and Country Club. Players of international reputation were entered in this event, and as a result, the play offered sensation after sensation. The tournament was won by Harry Davis, of the Presidio Golf Club, after a struggle in which he eliminated such stars as Chick Evans, H. Chandler Egan, Heinrich Schmidt, and Jack Neville. Davis met Schmidt in the finals of the event and won only after a dazzling exhibition of driving and putting such as has seldom been seen on a California course.

In addition to the men's championships, the women were in the limelight for a week. Miss Edith Chesebrough won the finals of the first flight play over Mrs. H. T. Baker. Mixed foursomes, events for professionals, driving, putting, and approaching contests were all included upon the programme, with gratifying results.

Yachting was granted an appropriate position upon the calendar, the races scheduled including yachts, sloops and motor boats upon San Francisco Bay and the ocean waters in the neighborhood of the Farallones. Perhaps the biggest event upon the programme is to be the International Regatta scheduled for August 1st to 31st, an event intended to bring into competition practically every type of racing craft afloat. This has brought attractive entries from both Eastern and Pacific clubs.

Special events were also arranged. A schooner race, with a course starting from a point on the bay off the Exposition and extending to the Farallone Islands, is one of them. Perhaps the most attractive of these events, however, will be the long-distance race for yachts from New York to San Francisco. The boats are to sail along the Atlantic seaboard, reaching San Francisco via the Panama Canal. Several entries for this contest have already been filed, and it is expected that by the time set for the start, a first class field will be ready to weigh anchor. Handsome cups, furnished by the Exposition for winners in the different nautical events, include many valuable trophies.

Boxing, the professional phase of which was recently abolished by an act of the California legislature, found an important place upon the Exposition programme. Amateur events staged at the Civic Auditorium excited great interest. By a special arrangement with the Amateur Athletic Union, the Exposition management obtained the national winners of Boston for the San Francisco tournament. Accordingly, the best of the country's amateur glove crop exhibited their wares to big galleries. In the matter of championships, California and the Pacific Northwest obtained the chief honors, several of the Eastern ring stars falling by the wayside in their work.

Not to be found wanting in the completeness of their scheme, the Exposition directors are still busy with plans which promise many events of unusual attractiveness for the Fall. It is hinted that the winner of the world's baseball series, waged between the National and American leagues, will be brought to the Coast for an exhibition series in October, to play against an all star team. Other phases of sport during the Exposition period include rowing, lawn tennis, handball and certain types of football, though disagreements between the two largest universities of the Coast have made the autumn sport an uncertain quantity.

Ben Macomber

XX.

The Joy Zone

A mile of amusement places, many of which are really educational - The Panama Canal, Grand Canyon, Yellowstone Park and the native villages - "The 101 Ranch" - "Toyland Grown Up" - Other notable features.

The Joy Zone, nearly a mile in length, is a broad avenue bordered with closely packed places of amusement. There are more than one hundred concessionaires, with two hundred and twenty buildings devoted to refreshment or pleasure, including a few in other places on the grounds. Here are all sorts of divertissements, from roller coasters to really great educational sights like the Panama Canal or the Grand Canyon.

By common consent the Panama Canal is the most noteworthy feature of the Zone. Indeed, it ought not to be on the Zone. It should have had a place in the Exposition proper, as one of its finest exhibits. The show is a working reproduction of the Panama Canal, on so large a scale that it covers five acres. The landscape of the Canal Zone is faithfully reproduced, with real water in the two oceans, the Gatun Lake, the Chagres River and the Canal. The visitor sees it from cars which travel slowly around the scene, and which are fitted with telephonic connections with a phonograph that explains the features of the Canal Zone as the appropriate points are passed. Next to seeing the Canal itself, a sight of this miniature is the most interesting and instructive view possible of the great engineering feat. In one way it is even better than a trip through the Canal. It gives the broad general view impossible from any point on the Isthmus itself.

In much the same class are the reproductions of the Grand Canyon and the Yelllowstone Park. The Grand Canyon has an added interest in the presence of Navajo and Hopi families living in reproductions of their desert homes. Representing other native races, there are the Samoan Village, the Maori Village, and the Tehuantepec Village. All these people are genuine and live in primitive style on the Zone, though, to tell the truth, they are quite likely to use college slang and know which fork to use first. Not on the Zone, but proper to be mentioned here, are the Blackfoot Indians brought to the Exposition from Glacier Park by the Great Northern Railroad. Eagle Calf is a real chief of the old days, and his band is a picturesque group.

There is Toyland Grown Up, a product of the astonishing genius of Frederic Thompson, creator of Luna Park, covering nearly twelve acres and packed with Thompson's whimsical conceptions of the figures of the Mother Goose Tales, Kate Greenway's children, and soldiers and giants, and the familiar toys of the Noah's Ark style-all on a gigantic scale. Japan Beautiful, a concession backed by the Japanese Government, has many interesting features, including the enormous gilded figure of Buddha over the entrance and a reproduction of Fujiyama in the

Ben Macomber

background. Then there is an Antarctic show entitled "London to the South Pole;" the Streets of Cairo; the Submarines, with real water and marine animals; Creation, a vast dramatic scene from Genesis; the Battle of Gettysburg; the Evolution of the Dreadnaught; and many other spectacles and entertainments of many classes, but all measuring up to a certain standard of excellence insisted upon by the Exposition. The Aeroscope, a huge steel arm that lifts a double decked cabin more than two hundred and fifty feet above the ground and then swings it around in a great circle over the Zone, is one of the thrillers.

The Joy Zone has suffered from the excellence of the Exposition to which it is the side-show. The Exposition itself is so wonderful a sight and contains so vast a number of remarkable and interesting things that multitudes have been content to stay with it, too much engrossed to find time for any but a few of the best things on the Zone. No better evidence could be found of the beauty, interest and value of this Exposition.

Appendix

(A) Sculptures and Mural Paintings

The following lists give the titles, locations and names of artists of the Exposition Sculptures and Mural Paintings. They do not include work exhibited in the Palace of Fine Arts, or in the state or foreign buildings, but only those which were designed for the adornment of the Exposition palaces, courts, and gardens.

The lists also index all matter and illustrations describing or showing this "Exposition art." Figures in light-face type refer to pages in the text; those in black-face type, to illustrations.

Ben Macomber

I.

Sculptures.

South Gardens. - Two Mermaid Fountains, by Arthur Putnam (21, 84, 99); Fountain of Energy, by A. Stirling Calder (83, 47).

Palace of Horticulture - Figures at bases of spires, by Eugene Louis Boutier; Pairs of Caryatids, by John Bateman (21).

Festival Hall. - The Torch Bearer (on domes), Bacchus, The Listening Woman, Flora and Pan, Flora and Dreaming Girl, Figures on cartouche over entrance, all by Sherry E. Fry (26, 26, 32).

Tower of Jewels. - Cortez (east side of arch), by Charles Niehaus (46, 48); Pizarro (west side of arch), by Charles C. Rumsey; Priest, Soldier, Philosopher and Adventurer, by John Flanagan (46, 44); Armored Horseman (on terrace of tower), by F. M. L. Tonetti (46); Fountain of Youth, by Edith Woodman Burroughs (49, 84, 89, 53); Fountain of El Dorado, by Gertrude Vanderbilt Whitney (49, 84, 89, 54).

Palace of Varied Industries. - Man with a Pick, Tympanum group of Varied Industries, New World Receiving Burdens of Old, Keystone figure, Power of

Industry, all by Ralph Stackpole (33, 37, 132); Victory (on the gables of all the central palaces), by Louis Ulrich (28, 18).

Palaces of Manufactures and Liberal Arts. - Frieze over Portals, Craftsmen, Woman with Spindle, Man with Sledgehammer, all by Mahonri Young (33).

Palace of Education. - Typanum group, Education, by Gustav Gerlach (34, 132); Panel, Male Teacher, by Cesare Stea; Panel, Female Teacher, by C. Peters (34).

West Facade of Palace Group. - Thought (on columns flanking half domes), by Ralph Stackpole; The Triumph of the Field, by Charles B. Harley; Abundance, by Charles R. Harley; Ex Libris (half dome of Education), by Albert Weinert; Physical Vigor (half dome of Food Products), by Earl Cummings; Vestibule Fountains, by W. B. Faville (all on p. 34, 35).

North Facade of Palace Group. - The Conquistador and The Pirate, both by Allen Newman (35, 43, 44).

East Facade of Palace Group. - The Miner, by Albert Weinert (35).

Column of Progress. - The Adventurous Bowman, by Herman A, MacNeil (56, 61, 57); The Burden Bearers (frieze at base of group), by Herman A. MacNeil (61); Frieze of Progress (frieze on pedestal), by Isidore Konti (61, 60).

Court of the Universe. - Nations of East and West (on arches), by A. Stirling Calder, Leo Lentelli and Frederick G. R. Roth (52, 65, 63, 59).

Genii on Columns, by Leo Lentelli; Pegasus Spandrels, by Frederick G. B. Roth; Medallions, by B. Bufano and A. Stirling Calder; The Stars, by A. Stirling Calder; Signs of the Zodiac, by Herman A. MacNeil (all on p. 52).

Fountains of the Rising and the Setting Sun, by A. A. Weinmann (52, 90, 63, 69); The Elements, Earth, Air, Fire and Water, by Robert Aitken (52, 64); Music and Poetry, by Paul Manship (52).

Court of the Ages. - Fountain of the Earth, by Robert Aitken (65, 66, 72, 91-5, 70, 73); Columns of Earth and Air, by Leo Lentelli (66, 67); Ages of Civilization (on Altar) and Thought (on side altars), by Chester Beach (66, 67, 70); Primitive Man, Primitive Woman, and The Hunter (on arcades), by Albert Weinert (66); Modern Time Listening to the Story of the Ages (in North Court), by Sherry E. Fry (67, 72).

Court of Seasons. - The Harvest (on half dome), by Albert Jaegers; Rain and Sunshine (on columns), by Albert Jaegers; Feast of the Sacrifice (on pylons), by Albert Jaegers (76, 79); Fountain groups, The Seasons, by Furio Piccirilli (75-6, 90-1, 94); Attic figures of Abundance, and spandrels, by August Jaegers; Fountain of Ceres (forecourt), by Evelyn Beatrice Longman (77, 91, 79).

Court of Flowers. - The Pioneer, by Solon Borglum (81, 97); Fountain of Beauty and the Beast, by Edgar Walter (81, 95, 100); Flower Girls (in niches), by A. Stirling Calder (87, 100); The Fairy (above Italian towers), by Carl Gruppe; Lions, by Albert Laessle.

Court of Palms. - The End of the Trail, by James Earle

Fraser (82, 96); Caryatids (on attic), by A. Stirling Calder and John Bateman; Spandrels (over portals), by Albert Weinert.

Palace of Machinery. - Genius of Creation, by Daniel Chester French (98, 147); Steam Power, Electricity, Imagination, Invention; Friezes, Genii of Machinery; Reliefs on bases of columns, Application of Power to Machines; all by Haig Patigian (97, 111); Eagles, by C. H. Humphries (97).

Palace of Fine Arts. - The Weeping Woman (on colonnade flower boxes), by Ulric H. Ellerhusen (102, 113); The Struggle for the Beautiful (three panels repeated on attic of Rotunda), by Bruno Louis Zimm (102, 114); Figures between panels, by Ulric H. Ellerhusen; Venus, Altar of Inspiration, by Ralph Stackpole (103, 197); Frieze of Genius (on Altar), by Bruno Louis Zimm; the Priestess of Culture (in Rotunda), by Herbert Adams (103); Aspiration (over main portal), by Leo Lentelli; Decorations on Flower Receptacles, by Ulric H. Ellerhusen (103).

II.

Mural Paintings.

Tower of Jewels. - West panel - Joining of Atlantic and Pacific, center; Discovery, left; Purchase, right. East panel - Gateway of All Nations, center; Labor Crowned, left; Achievement, right; all by William de Leftwich Dodge (46, 53).

Arch of the Nations of the East. - South panel - The Western March of Civilization; North panel - Ideals Attending Immigration; both by Edward Simmons (55-6).

Arch of the Nations of the West. - North panel - Pioneers Leaving for the West; South panel - Pioneers Arriving on Pacific Coast; both by Frank Vincent Du Mond (56, frontispiece).

Court of the Ages. - Earth, two panels (northwest corner of corridor); Air, two panels (southwest corner of corridor); Water, two panels (southeast corner of corridor); Fire, two panels (northeast corner of corridor); all by Frank Brangwyn (67, 68, 71, 74).

Court of Seasons. - Art Crowned by Time (in half dome); Man Receiving Instruction in Nature's Laws (in half dome); Spring and Seedtime (two panels in corridor before niche of Spring); Summer and Fruition (two panels In corridor before niche of Summer); Autumn and Harvest (two panels in corridor before niche of Autumn); Winter and Festivity (two panels in corridor before niche of Winter); all by H. Milton Bancroft (75, 76).

Court of Palms. - Fruits and Flowers (lunette over entrance of Palace of Education), by Childe Hassam; The Pursuit of Pleasure (lunette over entrance of Palace of Liberal Arts), by Charles Holloway; The Triumph of Culture, sometimes called The Victorious Spirit (lunette over entrance of Court of Seasons), by Arthur Mathews (all on p. 82).

Rotunda, Palace of Fine Arts. - The Conception and Birth of Art, four panels alternated with four panels of the Golds of California. In order they are: The Birth of European Art, the Orange Panel, Inspiration in All Art, the Wheat Panel, the Birth of Oriental Art, Metallic Gold, Ideals in Art, the Poppy Panel; all by Robert Reid (103, 104).

(B) Statistics of Construction Work

Palace	Size, feet	Exhibit area	Cost
Mines and Metallurgy	451 x 579	5.75 acres	$359,445
Transportation	579 x 614	7.25 acres	$481,677
Agriculture	579 x 639	7.5 acres	$425,610
Food Products	424 x 579	5.4 acres	$342,551

Ben Macomber

Varied Industries	414 x 541	5. acres	$312,691
Manufactures	475 x 552	5.35 acres	$341,069
Liberal Arts	475 x 585	5.75 acres	$344,180
Education	394 x 526	4.7 acres	$425,610
Machinery	972 x 372	9. acres	$659,665
Fine Arts	1100 x 186	5. acres	$580,000
Horticulture	672 x 329	5. acres	$341,000
Festival Hall	seats 4000		$270,000
Tower of Jewels 435 feet high			$428,000

Dome of Palace of Horticulture 185 feet high, 152 feet in diameter. Paved area within the Exposition grounds, 4,000,000 square feet, or 91.5 acres. At an average width of 40 feet, this is equal to nearly 20 miles of asphalt.

(C) The Exposition Roster

President. - Charles C. Moore.

Vice-Presidents. - William H. Crocker, Reuben B. Hale, I. W. Hellman, Jr., M. H. de Young, Leon Sloss, James Rolph, Jr.

Secretary. - Rudolph J. Taussig.

Treasurer. - A. W. Foster.

Board of Directors. - John Barneson, M. J. Brandenstein, John A. Britton, Frank L. Brown, George T. Cameron, Philip T. Clay, William H. Crocker, R. A. Crothers, M. H. de Young, A. I. Esberg, Charles S. Fee, H. F. Fortmann, A. W. Foster, H. B. Hale, I. W. Hellman, Jr., Homer S. King, Curtis H. Lindley, P. H. McCarthy, James McNab, Charles C. Moore, Thornwell Mullally, Dent H. Robert, James Rolph, Jr., A. W. Scott, Jr., Henry T. Scott, Leon Sloss, Charles S. Stanton, Rudolph J. Taussig, Joseph S. Tobin.

Executive Staff. - Director-in-Chief, Frederick J. V. Skiff; Director of Works, Harris D. H. Connick; Director of Exhibits, Asher Carter Baker; Director of Exploitation, George Hough Perry; Director of Concessions and Admissions, Frank Burt.

Architectural Commission. - George W. Kelham, San Francisco, Chief of Architecture; Willis Polk, William B. Faville, Clarence H. Ward, and Louis Christian Mullgardt, San Francisco; Robert Farquhar, Los Angeles; McKim, Mead & White, Carrere & Hastings, and Henry Bacon, New York. Associate Architects: Arthur Brown, Jr., G. Albert Lansburgh, Bernard R. Maybeck, San Francisco.

Division of Works. - Director, Harris D. H. Connick; Assistant Director of Works and Chief of Department of Construction, A. H. Markwart; Chief of Architecture, George W. Kelham; Chief, Department of Sculpture, K. T. F. Bitter; Acting Chief, A. Stirling Calder; Chief, Department of Color and Decoration, Jules Guerin; Chief, Department Civil Engineering, E.

Ben Macomber

E. Carpenter; Chief, Mechanical and Electrical Engineering, Guy L. Bayley; Chief, Department of Illumination, W. D'A. Ryan; Chief, Department of Landscape Gardening, John McLaren.

Division of Exhibits. - Director, Asher Carter Baker; Chief, Department of Fine Arts, John E. D. Trask; Assistant Chief, Department of Fine Arts, Robert B. Harshe; Chief, Department of Education and Social Economy, Alvin E. Pope; Chief, Department of Liberal Arts, Theodore Hardee; Chief, Department Manufactures and Varied Industries, Charles H. Green; Chief, Department of Machinery, George W. Danforth; Chief, Department of Transportation, Blythe E. Henderson; Chief, Department of Agriculture, Thomas G. Stallsmith; Chief, Department of Live Stock, D. O. Lively; Assistant Chief, Department of Live Stock, I. D. Graham; Chief, Department of Horticulture, G. A. Dennison; Chief, Department of Mines and Metallurgy, C. E. van Barneveld.

Other Department Heads. - Traffic Manager, Andrew M. Mortensen. General Attorney, Frank S. Brittain. Commandant of Exposition Guards, Captain Edward Carpenter, U. S. A. Director of Congresses, James A. Barr. Director of Music, George W. Stewart. Director of Special Events, Theodore Hardee. Chief of Special Events, Rolls E. Cooley. Chairman of Music Committee, J. J. Levison.

California State Commission. - Governor Hiram W. Johnson, ex officio; Matt I. Sullivan, President, San Francisco ; Chester H. Rowell, Fresno ; Marshall Stimson , Los Angeles ; Arthur Arlett, San Francisco. Commissioner General , W. D. Egilbert. Secretary, F. J. O'Brien. Controller, Leo

S. Robinson.

Woman's Board of the Exposition. - Honorary President, Mrs. Phoebe A. Hearst; President, Mrs. F. G. Sanborn; Vice-Presidents, Mrs. Lovell White, Mrs. I. Lowenberg, Mrs. W. H. Taylor, Mrs. John F. Merrill, Mrs. Frank L. Brown, Mrs. Irving M. Scott; Secretary, Mrs. Gaillard Stoney; Treasurer, Mrs. P. E. Bowles; Assistant Treasurer, Mrs. E. R. Dimond; Auditor, Mrs. Charles W. Slack. Directors, Mrs. Edson F. Adams, Mrs. Frank B. Anderson, Mrs. P. E. Bowles, Dr. Marian Bertola, Mrs. Frank L. Brown, Mrs. Aylett R. Cotton, Mrs. Francis Carolan, Mrs. Edwin R. Dimond, Mrs. Joseph A. Donohoe, Mrs. Joseph D. Grant, Mrs. Reuben B. Hale, Mrs. P. C. Hale, Mrs. Phoebe A. Hearst, Mrs. I. W. Hellman, Jr., Mrs. C. Edward Holmes, Mrs. John Johns, Mrs. Henry Krebs, Mrs. Jesse N. Lillenthal, Mrs. I. Lowenberg, Miss Laura McKinstry, Mrs. John F. Merrill, Mrs. Robert Oxnard, Mrs. Horace D. Pillsbury, Mrs. George A. Pope, Mrs. F. &. Sanborn, Mrs. Henry T. Scott, Mrs. Laurence Irving Scott, Mrs. William T. Sesnon, Mrs. Ernest G. Simpson, Mrs. Charles W. Slack, Mrs. M. C. Sloss, Mrs. Gaillard Stoney, Mrs. William Hinckley Taylor, Mrs. William S. Tevis, Mrs. Lovell White, Mrs. Edward Wright.

Foreign Commissioners

Argentina. - Horacio Anasagasti, Resident Commissioner General; Alberto M. D'Alkaine, Secretary.

Australia. - Alfred Deakin, Commissioner General, resigned; Niel Nielsen, New South Wales; F. W. Hagelthorn, Victoria; F. T. A. Fricke, Victoria, Deputy

Commissioner; J. A. Robertson, Queensland; George Oughton, Secretary.

Bolivia. - Manuel Vicente Ballivian, Commissioner General.

Canada. - William Hutchison. Canadian Exhibition Commissioner.

China. - Chen Chi, Resident Commissioner General; Allan S. Chow, Secretary.

Cuba. - General Enrique Loynaz del Castillo, Commissioner General; Dr. Amando Montero, Secretary.

Denmark. - Otto Wadsted, Resident Commissioner.

France. - Albert Tirman, Commissioner General; Jean Guyffrey, Secretary.

Guatemala. - Jose Flamenco, Resident Commissioner; Fernando Crux, Sec.

Honduras. - Antonio A. Ramirez F. Fontecha, Commissioner General; Fernando Somoza Vivas, Resident Commissioner.

Italy. - Ernesto Nathan, Commissioner General; Vito Catastini, Secretary.

Japan. - Haruki Yamawaki, Resident Commissioner General; Shinji Yoshino, Secretary.

Netherlands. - B. A. van Coenen Torchiana, Resident Commissioner.

New Zealand. - Edmund Clifton, Commissioner General; M. O'Brien, Sec.

Norway. - F. Herman Gade, Commissioner General; Birger A. Guthe, Sec.

Persia. - Mirza Ali Kuli Khan, Commissioner General.

Portugal. - Manuel Roldan, Commissioner General.

Siam. - James H. Gore, Commissioner General; A. H. Duke, Secretary.

Spain. - Count del Valle de Salazar, Representative.

Sweden. - Richard Bernstrom, Commissioner General; Herman Virde, Sec.

Turkey. - Vahan Cardashian, Imperial Adjutant High Commissioner.

Uruguay. - Eduardo Perotti, Commissioner General.

Commissioners From States and Islands

National Commission. - William Phillips, Chairman; Franklin D. Roosevelt, Judge W. B. Lamar; F. N. Bauskette, Secretary.

Arkansas. - F. B. T. Hollenberg, Commissioner General.

California. - Matt L Sullivan, President; W. D. Egilbert, Commissioner General; F. J. O'Brien, Secretary.

Ben Macomber

Hawaii. - R. P. Wood, Chairman.

Idaho. - Jay A. Czizek, Executive Commissioner.

Illinois. - Adolph Karpen, Chairman; Guy E. Cramer, Resident Executive; John G. Oglesby, Secretary.

Indiana. - S. P. Hamilton, Resident Commissioner.

Iowa. - W. W. Marsh, Chairman.

Kansas. - George H. Hodges, President; H. S. Dean, Secretary.

Maryland. - Roberdeau A. McCormick, Chairman; Robert J. Beachman, Sec.

Massachusetts. - Peter H. Corr, Chairman; Charles O. Power, Secretary.

Mississippi. - Isham Evans, Chairman; D. Ben Holmes, Secretary.

Missouri. - John L. McNatt, Chairman; Norman M. Vaughan, Secretary.

Montana. - David Hilger, Chairman; Frank A. Hazelbaker, Secretary.

Nevada. - George T. Mills, Commissioner.

New Jersey. - Robert S. Hudspeth, President; Charles F. Pancoast, Sec.

New York. - Norman E. Mack, Chairman; Daniel L. Ryan, Secretary.

North Dakota. - Governor L. B. Hanna, Chairman; Will E. Holbein, Sec.

Ohio. - D. B. Torpey, Resident Commissioner.

Oklahoma. - J. J. Dunn, Resident Commissioner; Mrs. Fred E. Sutton, Sec.

Oregon. - O. M. Clark, Chairman; George Ryland, General Manager.

Pennsylvania. - Martin G. Brumbaugh, President; A. G. Hetherington, Director in Charge; C. B. Carothers, Secretary.

Philippines. - Leon M. Guerrero, President; W. W. Barkley, Secretary.

Texas. - Mrs. Eli Hertzberg, Chairman; J. T. Bowman, Secretary.

Utah. - Glen Miller, Chairman; Mae Lail, Secretary.

Virginia. - W. W. Baker, Chairman; Alexander Forward, Secretary.

Washington. - John Schramm, President; Charles G. Heifner, Executive Commissioner.

West Virginia. - Paul Grosscup, Chairman; G. O. Nagle, Secretary.

Wisconsin. - John T. Murphy, Chairman; Arthur W. Prehn, Resident Commissioner; D. E. Bowe, Secretary.

Ben Macomber

(D) Bibliography

The Panama-Pacific Exposition presents so many aspects of public importance that it will doubtless inspire a considerable library of books upon its various features. Those heretofore published, however, agree in testifying to the unprecedented appeal which it makes on its artistic side; they have attempted little more than to describe the architecture of the main exhibit palaces, and interpret the Sculpture and murals which adorn them.

Of the titles given below, the first two volumes are wholly of this character. Mrs. James' little book has especial reference to the story told by the decorative Sculpture. The attractive Neuhaus volume is a more critical discussion of the Exposition art, as distinguished from exhibits in the Palace of Fine Arts, which are to be covered by Prof. Neuhaus' second book. To an outline of Exposition art, Mr. Cheney's booklet adds a brief, helpful account of the Fine Arts exhibit. Mr. Barry's more ambitious volume opens with an interesting chapter on the Exposition's inception and growth; the remainder of the text "is mainly devoted to the artistic features associated with the courts and the main palaces.".

The other books named describe and show "Exposition art."

Palaces and Courts of the Exposition, by Juliet James. 16mo., 151 pp.. including 32 illustrations. San Francisco, the California Book Co.

The Art of the Exposition, by Eugen Neuhaus. 8vo., 100 pp., with 32 ills. San Francisco, Paul Elder & Co.

An Art-Lover's Guide to the Exposition, by Sheldon Cheney. 12mo., 100 pp., including 20 ills. Berkeley, published by the author.

The City of Domes, by John D. Barry. 12mo., 142 pp., with 48 ills. San Francisco, J. J. Newbegin.

In the Court of the Ages (Poems), by Edward Robeson Taylor. 8vo., 33 pp., 7 ills. San Francisco, A. M. Robertson.

The Sculpture and Murals of the Panama-Pacific International Exposition, by Stella G. S. Perry. 12mo., 112 pp., including 47 ills. San Francisco, the Wahlgreen Co.

The Galleries of the Exposition, by Eugen Neuhaus. 8vo., 108 pp., with 30 ills. Paul Elder & Co.

The Sculpture of the Exposition Palaces and Courts, by Juliet James. 12mo., 32 ills. San Francisco, H. S. Crocker Co.

Ben Macomber

www.ingramcontent.com/pod-product-compliance
Lightning Source LLC
Chambersburg PA
CBHW031837170526
45157CB00001B/338